New

Poems

of

Emily

Dickinson

New

Poems *of*

Emily

Dickinson

Edited by William H. Shurr

with Anna Dunlap & Emily Grey Shurr

The University of North Carolina Press

Chapel Hill & London

G G H S

Contents

Preface, ix

1 ᴁ Introduction: The Metrics of the Letters, 1

2 ᴁ The Epigrams, 14

3 ᴁ New Poems, 38

4 ᴁ Tetrameters, Trimeters, Riddles, and Such, 64

5 ᴁ Workshop Materials, 84

6 ᴁ Juvenilia, Sources, and the Growth of the Poet, 92

7 ᴁ Bibliographical Essay, 103

Bibliography, 107

Index of Subjects, 111

Index of First Lines, 115

Preface

I wish to express my gratitude to the National Endowment for the Humanities, which awarded me funds for a project called "New Methods of Editing the Letters of Emily Dickinson." The John C. Hodges Fund of the University of Tennessee English Department has also provided help for the development of this project.

Thanks also to my two assistants. We have all studied the letters, and each of us has found poems that the others missed. All of us have participated in the research, the editorial decisions, and the many other chores that go into the making of a book. Thanks to my friends Suzanne Juhasz, Emory Elliott, and Everett Emerson for their support and encouragement of this work. Caroline Maun has also provided a careful reading and many good suggestions. And thanks finally to Carol Rigsby, who aided greatly in preparing the final version of the manuscript.

All of the new poems printed in this book are taken from Thomas H. Johnson's three-volume work, *The Letters of Emily Dickinson* (Cambridge: Harvard University Press, Belknap Press, 1955).

Each poem deemed to be a permanent addition to the Dickinson canon is given its own number on the far left. These numbers are for identification only and do not indicate chronological order. The source of each poem is noted in the text or in parentheses at the end by the Johnson number of the letter from which it was taken; this number will enable the reader to establish the chronological position of the work in the Dickinson canon and also to search out the context. Throughout, I have followed Johnson's rendition of Dickinson's spelling and punctuation.

A Letter is a joy of Earth—
It is denied the Gods—
Letter 960

Chapter One

Introduction: The Metrics
of the Letters

As readers of Emily Dickinson know, there are presently
1,775 poems in her canon. No additions have been made since the
1955 publication of Thomas H. Johnson's three-volume variorum
edition of the poems. This is surprising, because the expectation
when Johnson's work appeared was that the edition would gener-
ate a new and wider interest in Dickinson and that such publicity
would bring new materials to light. But though more than thirty-
five years have passed, no new troves of poetry or correspondence
have been discovered. Not a single scrap of significant new material
has emerged.

When Richard B. Sewall finished his biography of 1974, he listed
at the end a census of all known Dickinson correspondence that
had not yet been found. Not even this second stimulus has pro-
duced new materials, nor have the continuing research efforts of

Dickinson scholars who produce dozens of new books and essays each year. Yet we continue to hope that there are stores of Dickinson material still to be discovered, works to feed the appetite of those who would like to have more of her poems.

In the meantime—until some barn or attic yields its treasures—a source of new Dickinson poems does exist that has not yet been mined, though it has lain close at hand for many decades. I refer to Dickinson's letters and the prose-formatted poems she included in them. A careful excavation of these letters reveals many new poems and fragments of poems, poems which should be added to the canon and studied in their rightful place there.

As her readers know, Dickinson's letters are highly charged. Passages are nervous, intelligent, rhythmic, allusive, musical—as are the poems. She herself wrote out some passages as poetry; others echo with her typical and favored poetic devices. The present work is a study and presentation of these poetic materials in the three volumes of her letters.

The study has yielded nearly five hundred new poems which can be categorized into five types: first, Dickinson's epigrams, to be prized as a new genre never before identified; second, what I shall call "prose-formatted poems," passages from her letters which, when the format is altered, look very much like the Dickinson poems we are already familiar with; third, a group of miscellaneous poetic forms, including riddles; fourth, what seem to be rough drafts or workshop materials that appear in her letters as fragmentary poems; and fifth, a collection of juvenilia from her early letters which gives some unexpected glimpses into the sources of her style. These categories determine the five major chapters of this book. Each category will be discussed at greater length in the appropriate chapter.

The poems in this collection were mostly written out as prose in Dickinson's letters, except for the very few clearly indicated citations of previously established poems included by Johnson in the *Complete Poems* and introduced here for comparison.

In preparing his edition of Dickinson's poems, Johnson carefully studied the manuscript drafts of her letters, searching for those poems that "look like" poems on the written page, with each line indented from the left. He included most of them in *The Poems of Emily Dickinson* (3 vols., 1955) and *The Complete Poems of Emily Dickinson* (1960). But this methodology left behind many Dickinson poems disguised in the letters as prose. Numerous passages in the letters fall into Dickinson's easily recognized "fourteeners," a line of iambic tetrameter followed by a line of iambic trimeter. This is the ballad meter or hymn meter (also called "common measure" in the hymnbooks) which was Dickinson's line of choice. When she thought "writing," she frequently thought "fourteeners." During many years of listening to Emily Dickinson's poetry, I have come to think of this formation as a part of her poetic signature. Other elements of her signature—the use of a dash for a pause, the use of initial capitals to emphasize words, and her idiosyncratic use of "it's" as a possessive (her lifelong campaign to legitimize this usage never prevailed)—have also aided in the search for the proper poems to excavate. All of these devices have frequently signaled a poem hidden in the prose text.

Some readers may object that these methods for editing Dickinson have no precedent, that changing her prose lines to poetry is too radical an editorial tactic. This is not true. I have not done anything that Thomas H. Johnson or, more important, that Dickinson herself did not do.

Johnson, for example, isolated an obviously prose-formatted poem and published it as one of Dickinson's earliest works of poetry. The poem appears in its original prose format in letter 58. Johnson published it thus as number 2 of the *Complete Poems*:

> There is another sky,
> Ever serene and fair,
> And there is another sunshine,
> Though it be darkness there;
> Never mind faded forests, Austin,
> Never mind silent fields—
> *Here* is a little forest,
> Whose leaf is ever green;
> Here is a brighter garden,
> Where not a frost has been;

In its unfading flowers
I hear the bright bee hum;
Prithee, my brother,
Into *my* garden come!

No one has ever questioned the status of these lines as a poem, though they were formatted by Dickinson as prose. In printing the passage as a poem, Johnson took several liberties with Dickinson's original letter: first, he reformatted the lines from prose to poetry; second, he broke into the middle of Dickinson's grammatical sentence to begin his poem; and finally, he provided initial capitals for each of the lines. He reformatted several more poems from prose to poetry in the same way. Johnson himself thus furnishes a precedent for reformatting Dickinson's letter poems, and in a manner less conservative than the one I have adopted. I have not added or omitted any words, nor have I made any changes other than the addition of an occasional period at the end or initial capital at the beginning of a poem. With the exception of spacing, the poems are presented just as Dickinson wrote them. Where she wrote them as prose, I have printed them in her usual poetic lines.

More important than Johnson's precedent is the poet's own editorial practice in her letters. It is of the greatest interest to note that she frequently printed the same words indifferently as poetry or as prose. In a letter of 2 January 1885, for example, Dickinson incorporated the poem "Take all away from me" by indenting it and placing it between two prose statements. Apparently in this instance she wanted no mistake about the fact that the lines were poetry. And in a letter to her friend Helen Hunt Jackson (976), which Johnson dates a few months later that year, she included the same poem, also indented and separated from the prose portions of the letter. But in letter 1014, she takes the first two lines of the poem and blends them into her second paragraph as prose—with no indentations or other marks to signify that the lines had ever existed as poetry or that they were meant to be read as poetry. In Dickinson's own practice, then, the border between the two genres was easily permeable, and lines were portable from letter to letter.

This example suggests not only that Dickinson herself could be indifferent as to whether she wrote out her poems in their traditional format or as prose, but also that her poems had a kind of separate existence apart from the particular letters in which they might be imbedded, since she could move them around among quite different contexts. The evidence of the letters suggests further that Dickinson kept stores of finished poetry which she had no intention of publishing in the usual printed media but which she could mine when needed for a letter. Some of these she formatted as poems in her letters; the majority of these have already been identified and published by Johnson. Others she wrote out in a prose format. Occasionally she included different versions of the same poem in different letters and in different formats. Dickinson herself, in other words, cited her words "out of context" and was indifferent to their formatting.

One of her early letters to Susan Gilbert (173), who would soon become her sister-in-law, provides still another example of Dickinson's own editing practice. She wrote out the whole of the five-stanza poem "I have a Bird in spring," and Johnson published it as number 5 in the *Complete Poems*. But around the same time she wrote out the last stanza as prose in a letter to her good friend Mrs. Holland (175).

Letter 200, written when Dickinson was nearing 30, seems to hint that she herself was thinking of some connections between poems and her prose letters. The following prose lines can easily be formatted as poetry, as her typical stanza of two fourteeners:

1.   She [Lavinia Dickinson] talked of you before she went—
      often said she missed you,
      would add a couplet of her own,
      were she but at home.

Perhaps the quatrain deserves only a minor place in Dickinson's "canon"; but it is important to note that when Dickinson wrote she frequently fell into fourteeners, and that when she described prose, it was sometimes in poetic terms (in this case, with the word "couplet"). The prose lines furnish still another instance of the evanescence of the borderline between the two genres in Dickinson's practice.

The letters contain many other examples of her writing the same words sometimes as poetry and sometimes as prose. "Take all away from me," published in Johnson's *Complete Poems* as number 1640, was written in letters 960 and 976 as poetry, then in 1014 as prose. And in a distinctly unfriendly letter to Susan (173) she wrote out a long poem of five stanzas, which Johnson printed as such. Then in an affectionate letter to her traveling friends, the Hollands, she wrote a *prose* version that merges elements of stanzas 3 and 5. If reformatted as poetry, this passage seems different enough from the previous version to stand by itself as a new poem:

2.   Then will I not repine,
        knowing that bird of mine,
        though flown—
        learneth beyond the sea,
        melody new for me,
        and will return. (175)

Dickinson's practice was similar in all the different eras of her life. In the spring of 1877 she enclosed a poem in a letter to Mrs. Thomas Wentworth Higginson (498); she then sent the same poem to the family of her pastor, who was departing for a new church (499). It was printed in *Complete Poems* as number 1391. Once again, Dickinson's practice makes it apparent that a letter-poem is freestanding, not totally dependent on a single context.

Similarly, the epigram I have chosen to head the present chapter was written out as a poem by Dickinson, and Johnson printed it in *Complete Poems* as number 1639:

A Letter is a joy of Earth—
It is denied the Gods— (960)

But a few days later, in letter 963, she wrote virtually the same words as prose: "but a Letter is a joy of Earth—it is denied the

Gods." Obviously, Dickinson manipulated her poems from letter to letter. In this case, she added one word, capitalized others, and changed a dash to a period.

In still another example, the quatrain "Pass to thy Rendezvous of Light," which Johnson published as poem number 1564, was written as a poem into two separate letters, first to Susan Dickinson in 1883 (868) and again in a letter to Higginson two years later (972). Clearly Dickinson herself lifted her poems from one context to another quite freely. These examples should warn the critic against arbitrarily freezing her words too rigidly into the context of a particular letter.

Especially telling is the following poem, formatted as prose and sent in 1882 to James D. Clark, a friend of the Reverend Charles Wadsworth ("my dearest earthly friend," she called him in letter 807):

3. A Letter always seemed to me
  like Immortality,
  for is it not the Mind alone,
  without corporeal friend? (788)

Thirteen years earlier, in 1869, the same words (except that "seemed" was "feels" and the question was cast as a statement) had been sent to Thomas Wentworth Higginson, in letter 330. Here is an indubitable instance of a prose-formatted poem that had a long life apart from the fixed context of a particular letter.

Dickinson's practice thus suggests that some of the poems we have excavated were preexisting and freestanding works and that they can justifiably be printed separately. Yet another example leads to the same conclusions. Two letters dated by Johnson "about 1881" contain almost identical versions of the same poem, written out as prose in each instance:

4. Amazing human heart,
  a syllable can make
  to quake like jostled tree,
  what infinite for thee? (710)

5. Amazing Human Heart—
    a syllable can make
    to quake like jostled Tree—
    what Infinite—for thee! (715)

The words are identical, but I would argue for two entirely different poems here. The change in terminal punctuation changes the statement from a weak question to a strong affirmation, creating two separate poems from the same words. Dickinson also experiments here with changes in pace (through dashes) and emphasis (through capitalization). These prose-formatted passages, in other words, show a poem still in swift development, as if it had some status of its own apart from the two letters in which it appears.

The same phenomenon can be observed in another case. In a letter to her mentor Thomas Wentworth Higginson, Dickinson expresses the hope that he will visit her in Amherst and then asks in a fourteener which she formatted as prose:

6. Is this the Hope that opens and shuts,
    like the eye of the Wax Doll? (553)

In the same month, according to Johnson's dating, she was reworking this fourteener into a different poem, this time to her sister-in-law Susan:

7. This is the World that opens and shuts,
    like the Eye of the Wax Doll— (554)

The change of a key word changes the subject of the second poem, as does the change in terminal punctuation. Once again, Dickinson's poems have a fluid life beyond their static "contexts."

Another set of poems leads to the same conclusion. The following lines were written as prose to two different correspondents at around the same time. Here Dickinson is obviously experimenting to see which has the better rhythmic structure. One is a fourteener that seems to read slowly and meditatively; the other, a set of trimeters that seems more urgent:

8.   Home itself is far from home
       since my father died. (433)

9.   Home is so far from Home,
       since my Father died. (441)

In some of his notes Johnson opens a window into Dickinson's methods as a letter writer. It appears from his notes to letters 938, 974, and 976—to cite only a few examples—that Dickinson usually wrote at least one preliminary draft of her letters before sending the finished version. Parts of three separate drafts for a letter to Helen Hunt Jackson are extant (976). In her biography of Dickinson, Cynthia Griffin Wolff notes several other instances where phrases are repeated with variations from letter to letter and concludes that Dickinson "often . . . made preliminary drafts of her correspondence" (128), that "she was making first drafts of much of her correspondence. . . . Far from working haphazardly, Dickinson had begun to keep some sort of file or record of her work" (575). All of these examples suggest that the final versions of her letters might have been consciously composed from materials at hand, including her stores of poems.

One further set of examples, cited by Cristanne Miller, should be brought forward. Miller notices that Dickinson sent the same poem, printed in Johnson's *Complete Poems* as 792, both to Samuel Bowles and to Susan Dickinson. This intensely anguished poem— "Through the strait pass of suffering / The Martyrs—even— trod"—works well in the context of either letter. In fact, according to Miller, "In the letter to Sue, the poem would seem to have a different reference and perhaps significance. The poem expresses a truth Dickinson values and finds useful" ("'A Letter,'" 33). Miller also mentions the several versions of 494, "Going to Him! [Her!] Happy Letter," to make the point that a Dickinson letter-poem can exist "beyond any personal use she may put it to [in a particular letter]" ("'A Letter,'" 34).

To give a final example, Johnson did not include the following lines in his edition of Dickinson's poems, although she formatted them as poetry:

10. Show me Eternity, and I will show you Memory—
    Both in one package lain
    And lifted back again—
    Be Sue—while I am Emily—
    Be next—what you have ever been—Infinity— (912)

I believe these lines can stand also with the works published in her
Complete Poems. It is my intent to recover poems like these for
Dickinson's canon. The borders between Dickinson's poetry and
prose, between her poems and their contexts, are quite moveable,
and editing practices should take into account her actual practice.

There seems to be ample justification, then, for assuming that at
least some of the poems I present here originally enjoyed the status
of freestanding, contextless productions. As a matter of fact, the
epigrams and poems in the present edition were selected because
they easily exist apart from their the context in the letters. Detached
from their prose context, the proverbs seem even more brilliant,
more wise, more generally applicable. They transcend their origi-
nal contexts. In order further to isolate them for study, I have
organized them by genre rather than by chronology.

Instead of wondering about the propriety of quoting "out of
context," the reader may wish to ponder the opposing case: that the
epigrams and poems which are excavated and presented below are
too overwhelmed by their contexts in the letters. Dickinson did
many things with her texts, publishing them in her own way and in
various forms and arrangements in these letters. She chose no
other outlet for publication, and it is questionable whether the
letters—written to specific individuals concerned with the min-
utiae of everyday life—are really suitable context for these poems.
They seem to transcend such limiting contexts. It is only when they
are isolated and presented as freestanding poems that we can focus
on them as the works of art they are.

To those who would question the wisdom of "taking words
from context," there are two answers. The practical justification is
quite simple: doing so isolates some segments of her work for our
greater astonishment and for closer study as independent works.
The technical answer points out that she did it herself—changing

sections around and rewriting them, even reformatting some of them as poetry—and her best editor did the same.

One might also object that these poetic lines are not truly professional poems, that they are not sufficiently "public" in their provenance to be considered on the same level as her other poems. But we must remember that many if not most of Dickinson's poems were occasional, equally private, similarly "addressed" to a specific person. In fact, there is evidence to suggest that all of the poems of the fascicles—roughly half of the present canon—were written to one specific addressee alone, as I argued some years ago in *The Marriage of Emily Dickinson*.

Some of the problems I faced in completing the present edition have been solved by using suggestions from the work of Jerome McGann. McGann has pointed out interesting similarities between the texts of William Blake and Emily Dickinson. Blake engraved and printed each of his poems and then colored them by hand, sometimes with the help of his wife. He produced thereby a small number of "copies" of each poem, but each one was distinguished by unique differences. Dickinson's poems and letters, of course, were also unique and handcrafted texts. Editors of Dickinson and Blake thus face some of the same problems in bringing their works before the public (*Beauty of Inflections*, 119). The classic editorial principle, espoused by the Modern Language Association as late as 1985—to produce a text as close as possible to "the author's final intention" (Williams and Abbott, 58)—clearly cannot be carried out; in each case the author "intended" to produce one unique version at a time. So far as we can tell, neither poet ever intended to see works struck off in thousands of identical copies to be purchased and read by any consumer with the means and inclination to obtain them in book form. "When we edit we change," writes McGann, "and even good editing . . . necessarily involves fundamental departures from 'authorial intention,' however that term is interpreted" (*Textual Condition*, 53). The editor who insists on adhering to an older theory of editing stands thus at a crippling impasse.

To break this impasse, McGann suggests, the editor must bring other principles into play to mirror the fluid practice of editing and reediting as it actually takes place over a period of time, in order to fulfill changing social conditions and historical needs. McGann has described his work, in fact, as "a project to reintroduce a comprehensive socio-historical method into the study of literary texts." He encourages the editor to join most contemporary critics in recognizing "a poem's changing life in human society" (*Beauty of Inflections*, vii, 121). This principle suggests that editing must take into account the perceived needs of a present audience as well as the literary insights of the editor who is working on the text. It is along these more liberating or even transgressive lines that these new poems of Emily Dickinson are presented.

The best justification for this method of editing, however, will be the new poems themselves. As a prime example of the worth of these newly excavated poems, I offer the following. The reader familiar with Dickinson's poetry will recognize the voice and style. Though the poem seems to go slightly prosaic in the third and fourth lines, the last two lines redeem it entirely. Whether written specifically for a letter or imported from a preexisting supply, this poem is well worth detaching from the letters and elevating into the canon:

11.   Parting is one of the exactions
        of a Mortal Life.
        It is bleak—like Dying,
        but occurs more times.

        To escape the former,
        some invite the last.
        The Giant in the Human Heart
        was never met outside. (399)

The poems in this volume are authentic additions to the canon of Dickinson's poetry. The epigrams seem especially important in that they display in great numbers a type of poetry with which Dickinson has never been particularly identified. The new poems are also valuable as works of great beauty. In some cases they introduce new themes into the canon; in others they offer a further *approfon-dissement* of existing themes. They all provide the reader with greater certainty about dating than is now possible for many of the canonical poems; and they all add to the delight of the reader who will welcome a new trove of Dickinson poems.

Chamfort had been for many years in the habit of writing, each day, on little squares of paper the fruits of his reflections, reduced to maxims; the anecdotes he had gleaned; the events, illustrative of the history of manners, that he had witnessed in society; and the piquant epigrams and brilliant repartees he had heard or had perpetrated himself.
   P. N. Firbank, "A Double Life"

Chapter Two
The Epigrams

In this chapter I would like to introduce a new genre among the poems of Emily Dickinson: her freestanding fourteener epigrams. To my knowledge this form has never been isolated in her work, nor has she received serious or extended attention as one of the major epigrammatists in the language.

The word derives from the Greek *epigramma*—"in-scribed"—and suggests the short meaningful saying that can be carved on a tombstone or monument. The term has traditionally stood for several different kinds of expression. It has always designated a statement that is short and insightful; it is often considered part of a nation's inherited "wisdom." Sometimes the word is used loosely to include all kinds of proverbs and aphorisms. Such forms are prominent in the Upanishads and also in Russian and German collections. The saying "An Englishman's house is his castle" may be a permanent part of our mental furniture. The statement has the ring of the typical proverb. But no matter how memorable the saying is or how deeply it has sunk into the collective wisdom of the tribe, I still do not want to categorize it or sayings like it as epigrams. In labeling these new Dickinson poems *epigrams* I aim for a narrower definition of the word. For this purpose, an epigram is more fully poetry—figurative and metrical as well as memorable. M. H. Abrams once defined the epigram as any very short poem which is polished, terse, and pointed. It can be amatory, elegiac, meditative, complimentary, anecdotal, or satiric (54). The word "poem" is important here and persists in most descriptions. The short wise saying is more prized when cast in rhythm and rhyme. The types of epigrams Abrams lists are all to be found among Dickinson's epigrams.

If we were to include all of Dickinson's examples of terse wit—her proverbs in the broader sense—such items as the following, and many more, would be included: "Common Sense is almost as omniscient as God" (PF 68) and "Nothing is so old as a dilapidated charm—" (PF 94). These are both from the "prose fragments" printed by Johnson at the end of his third volume of Dickinson's letters. But I would like to set the bar higher, at least for this chapter, and present only those Dickinson epigrams that she set in hymn meter and in figurative language. The epigrams I have culled from her letters for this section all fall into that more demanding genre. The other criterion for their inclusion will be their ability to stand alone, independent of context.

Historically, some of the most exquisitely wrought epigrams are to be found in the *Greek Anthology*, a compilation of works by many authors from antiquity, brilliantly mined by a Dickinson successor, the poet H.D. The *Greek Anthology* established a tradition of verse that was polished, short, and elegant. The favored metrical form was the elegiac couplet, in which—as in Dickinson's fourteeners—a shorter line follows a longer. In contrast, the Latin tradition, represented by the poet Martial (A.D. 40–104), bent the epigram in a more vernacular direction, toward coarseness and harsh satire. In this tradition the epigram usually carries a barb. John Wilmot, Earl of Rochester, is a good representative of the English tradition descended from Martial:

We have a pretty witty King,
Whose word no man relies on,
Who never said a foolish thing,
Nor ever did a wise one.

The King's reputed answer to Lord Rochester—that his words were his own, while his acts were those of his ministers—is also sometimes called an epigram, but it lacks any of the traditional qualities of poetry.

John Owen, whose skills as an epigrammatist were highly regarded in his native Wales, exemplifies the strength and wisdom of the English epigram in its fully developed form. Jon Manchip White quotes him thus:

Thou ask'st what years thou hast? I answer None:
For what thou had'st, thou hast not: they be gone.

(White, 249)

Obviously the epigram can be solemn, elegant, and formal. Walter Savage Landor is famous for this kind of epigram, as in his lines "On His Seventy-Fifth Birthday":

I strove with none: for none was worth my strife,
Nature I loved, and next to Nature, Art;
I warmed both hands before the fire of life,
It sinks, and I am ready to depart.

The force of these epigrams is clearly heightened by the use of rhythm, rhyme, and figures of speech.

The English epigram of the classical era (1596–1616) followed something of the biblical model: the first part stated the occasion or set the tone, and a conclusion sharply and tersely gave the main point. A famous collection was published by Sir John Harington in 1615. For many, Ben Jonson is the premier English epigrammatist of this period. However, the English epigram reached a high point in the eighteenth century and is best exemplified in Alexander Pope's poetry, as in the following couplet from the *Essay on Criticism*:

We think our fathers fools, so wise we grow;
Our wiser sons, no doubt, will think us so.

One of the standard handbooks of literature observes that "many of Pope's couplets are epigrams *when separated from their context*" (Holman, 197, emphasis added), a statement that lends courage for the present enterprise.

Matthew Prior, another of England's best epigrammatists, can be represented by the following:

Sir, I admit your general rule,
That every poet is a fool:
But you yourself may serve to show it,
That every fool is not a poet.

And this epigram, called "On a Volunteer Singer," comes from Coleridge:

Swans sing before they die—'twere no bad thing
Should certain people die before they sing!

The epigram also came to Dickinson from other sources. When the Anglican bishop Robert Lowth first noticed the parallelism in Hebrew poetry, especially in Psalms and Proverbs, he added a distinctly different source for the genre. His lectures, published in 1753 as *The Sacred Poetry of the Hebrews*, acknowledged that the poetry of the Jewish Scriptures does not have meter in the sense familiar to English readers. Rather, the technique that signaled poetry was the grouping of coherent or self-contained sections of two or three lines, with the same number of stressed syllables per line. The statements within a single proverb are parallel and can be synonymous, antithetical, or cumulative. Proverbs 10:5 captures this form especially well:

The rich man's wealth is his stronghold,
poverty is the poor man's undoing.

Each line has three stresses, though the meter is loose by any model. The antithesis is striking, and a chiasmus is added to make the lines more memorable. In a similar vein:

> A wise son is his father's joy,
> A foolish son is his mother's grief.
>   (Proverbs 10:1)

The following four-stress lines are an especially good example of parallelism in the Psalms:

> The heavens declare the glory of God,
> The vault of heaven declares his handiwork.
>   (Psalm 19)

Many of Dickinson's epigrams seem to come directly from this source. The following, for example, was printed by Johnson among Dickinson's prose fragments in his third volume of her letters:

12.   Consummation is the hurry of fools,
       but Expectation the Elixir of the Gods— (PF 69)

In May of 1860 Dickinson wrote a letter of congratulations to Susan Davis Phelps for her engagement:

13.   'When thou goest through the Waters,
       I will go with thee.' (221)

The simple note is obviously a fourteener and a variation on a passage from Isaiah (43:2). Interestingly, the Isaiah original is also a fourteener: "When thou passeth through the waters, I will be with thee."

The literature of her own continent provided Dickinson with still another source of inspiration for her epigrams. She is obviously a literary descendant of Benjamin Franklin's Poor Richard. His epigrams are also characterized by rhythm and rhyme, though of a rougher sort:

An apple a day
keeps the doctor away.
A stitch in time
saves nine.

Deeper still in her background are the "Meditations Divine and Morall" of Anne Bradstreet, pithy and profound, though not in verse form.

Thus the epigrammatic style with formal poetic characteristics converges in Dickinson from sources such as the classical tradition, the English epigram, and the King James Bible, as well as the frequently remarked vernacular tradition of the ballad and the hymn. For wit, compactness and profound insight, Dickinson's epigrams easily stand comparison with examples from these four strands. They elevate Dickinson even more clearly to a position among the wisest of our writers and constitute one of American literature's major Books of Wisdom. They present a far more serious contender for that prize than the sayings of Poor Richard.

Dickinson was not unaware that she was composing epigrams. Early in her correspondence with Higginson she framed two fine epigrams and wrote them out as poetry in a letter to him (280). Johnson noted that they were poetry and published them in the *Complete Poems* as number 684,

Best Gains—must have the Losses' Test—
To constitute them—Gains—

and number 685,

Not "Revelation"—'tis—that waits,
But our unfurnished eyes—

But many other fourteener epigrams have not yet been noticed. An example appears in the third of the "Master letters":

14.   No Rose, yet felt myself a'bloom,
       No Bird—yet rode in Ether. (233)

Dickinson indicated by a caret mark that these lines should be inserted from the bottom of the page, as if the lines were a free-standing fragment.

The following lines appear in letter 288, formatted as prose:

15.   There is no first, or last, in Forever—
It is Centre, there, all the time—

This is one of her early experiments in the fourteener epigram. The parallel parenthetical commas, the capitalization of key words in each line, and the characteristic dashes are all part of her artistry.

A fourteener proverb written to her cousin Louise Norcross explores the possibilities of a dust / dew opposition:

16.   We all have moments with the dust,
but the dew is given. (337)

She seems to assert here that the life-giving forces are more permanent than thoughts of death. The same opposition of *dust* and *dew* proved useful in another fourteener epigram much later, with a new configuration of the same imagery:

17.   Success is dust, but an aim
forever touched with dew. (898)

In another letter the following prose-formatted epigram appears as grim commentary on the Victorian middle-class notion of the wife as the "angel in the house":

18.   Many an angel, with its needle,
toils beneath the snow. (435)

The epigram below also deserves to stand alone:

19.   Is it Intellect that the Patriot means
when he speaks of his "Native Land"? (413)

A profound fourteener epigram was printed by Johnson as one of Dickinson's prose fragments:

20.   The Blood is more showy (gaudy) than the Breath.
        But cannot dance as well— (PF 107)

The epigram seems to achieve insight by positing some fundamental opposition between body and spirit, between biological processes and human speech.

The rest of Dickinson's fourteener epigrams, newly excavated from the letters, are presented here without commentary.

21.   Not all of life to live, is it,
        nor all of death to die. (176)

22.   "They say that absence conquers."
        It has vanquished me. (176)

23.   Who knows where our hearts go,
        when this world is done? (180)

24.   Hereafter, I will pick no Rose,
        lest it fade or prick me. (189)

25.   Some time is longer than the rest,
        and some is very short. (194)

26.   We would'nt mind the sun, dear,
        if it did'nt *set*— (194)

27.   Many can boast a hollyhock,
        but few can bear a *rose*! (203)

28.   That *Bareheaded life*—under the grass—
        worries one like a Wasp. (220)

29. The love of God may be taught
    not to seem like bears. (230)

30. You might not know I remembered you,
    unless I told you so— (236)

31. Cages—do not suit the *Swiss*—
    well as steeper Air. (242)

32. I think it sad to have a friend—
    it's sure to break the Heart. (243)

33. I could not weigh myself—Myself—
    My size felt small—to me— (261)

34. I wish one could be sure the suffering
    had a loving side. (263)

35. The Sailor cannot see the North—
    but knows the Needle can— (265)

36. It's fragrant news, to know they pine,
    when we are out of sight. (266)

37. Had I a pleasure you had not,
    I could delight to bring it. (268)

38. It is easier to look behind at a pain,
    than to see it coming. (272)

39. The heart is the only workman
    we cannot excuse. (273)

40. Friends are nations in themselves—
    to supersede the Earth— (277)

41. Life is death we're lengthy at,
     death the hinge to life. (281)

42. I am sure I feel as Noah did,
     docile, but somewhat sceptic. (286)

43. I had hoped to express more.
     Love more I never can. (307)

44. November always seemed to me
     the Norway of the year. (311)

45. I notice where Death has been introduced,
     he frequently calls. (311)

46. Nature, seems it to myself,
     plays without a friend. (319)

47. The "infinite Beauty"—of which you speak
     comes too near to seek. (319)

48. The soul must go by Death alone,
     so, it must by life. (321)

49. Awkward as the homely are
     who have not mental beauty. (321)

50. Not a flake assaults my birds
     but it freezes me. (329)

51. Think of that great courageous place
     we have never seen! (329)

52. Gratitude is the timid wealth
     of those who have nothing. (330)

53. My life has been too simple and stern
     to embarrass any. (330)

54. Dying is a wild Night
     and a new Road. (332)

55. The Bird would be a soundless thing
     without Expositor. (333)

56. The things of which we want the proof
     are those we knew before— (334)

57. Who knows how deep the Heart is
     and how much it holds? (338)

58. The incredible never surprises us
     because it is the incredible. (342)

59. Oh Matchless Earth—We underrate
     the chance to dwell in Thee. (347)

60. Landscapes reverence the Frost,
     though it's gripe be past. (351)

61. I remember your coming as serious sweetness
     placed now with the Unreal— (352)

62. The Risks of Immortality
     are perhaps its' charm— (353)

63. How lonesome to be an Article!
     I mean—to have no soul. (354)

64. What Miracles the News is!
     Not Bismark but ourselves. (354)

65. Delight has no Competitor,
so it is always most. (355)

66. Love is that one perfect labor
nought can supersede. (357)

67. Why the Thief ingredient accompanies all Sweetness
Darwin does not tell us. (359)

68. That Possession fairest lies
that is least possest. (359)

69. Transport's mighty price is
no more than he is worth— (359)

70. The will is always near, dear,
though the feet vary. (360)

71. To live lasts always, but to love
is firmer than to live. (364)

72. No heart that broke but further went
than Immortality. (364)

73. It is the Meek that Valor wear
too mighty for the Bold (377)

74. We must be careful what we say.
No bird resumes its egg. (379)

75. The career of flowers differs from ours
only in inaudibleness. (388)

76. Science will not trust us
with another World. (395)

77.   I thought to shun the Loneliness
      that parting ratifies. (397)

78.   The Minor Toys of the Year are alike,
      but the Major—are different. (412)

79.   I thought that being a Poem one's self
      precluded the writing Poems. (413)

80.   You have experienced Sanctity.
      It is to me untried. (413)

81.   For the comprehension of Suffering
      One must ones Self have Suffered. (416)

82.   Had you an Hour unengrossed,
      it would be almost priceless. (418)

83.   Trial as a Stimulus
      far exceeds Wine. (428)

84.   Please rest the Life so many own,
      for Gems abscond— (438)

85.   Nature must be too young to feel,
      or many years too old. (442)

86.   My family of Apparitions
      is select, though dim. (445)

87.   There is nothing sweeter than Honor, but Love,
      which is it's sacred price. (449)

88.   Fear—like Dying, dilates trust,
      or enforces it— (453)

89. I raise only robins on my farm
and a blossom is quite a guest. (454)

90. It is delicate that each Mind is itself,
like a distinct Bird— (457)

91. It is still as distinct as Paradise—
the opening your first Book— (458)

92. Silence' oblation to the Ear
supersedes sound— (458)

93. Good times are always mutual;
that is what makes good times. (471)

94. The unknown is the largest need
of the intellect. (471)

95. It is of Realms unratified
that Magic is made. (472)

96. "We thank thee Oh Father" for these strange Minds,
that enamor us against thee. (472)

97. Death is perhaps an intimate friend,
not an enemy. (478)

98. Her reluctances are sweeter
than other ones' avowals. (479)

99. I thought your approbation Fame—
and it's withdrawal Infamy. (486)

100. I hope you are joyful frequently,
these beloved Days. (503)

101.   How strange that Nature does not knock,
       and yet does not intrude! (510)

102.   You asked me if I wrote now?
       I have no other Playmate— (513)

103.   You see we keep a jealous Heart—
       That is Love's Alloy— (520)

104.   How precious Thought and Speech are!
       "A present so divine." (521)

105.   Is not the distinction of Affection,
       almost Realm enough? (525)

106.   The immortality of Flowers
       must enrich our own. (528)

107.   Sorrow almost resents love,
       it is so inflamed. (536)

108.   Where we owe so much it defies Money,
       we are blandly insolvent. (541)

109.   Adulation is inexpensive
       except to him who accepts it. (541)

110.   Dear Mr Bowles found out too late,
       that Vitality costs itself. (542)

111.   The love which comes without aspect,
       and without herald goes. (545)

112.   "This tabernacle" is a blissful trial,
       but the bliss predominates. (551)

113.   I hope your rambles have been sweet
       and your reveries spacious— (553)

114.   Whatever await us of Doom or Home,
       we are mentally permanent. (555)

115.   Save me from the idolatry
       which would crush us both— (560)

116.   That Sorrow dare to touch the Loved
       is a mournful insult— (564)

117.   The tiniest ones are the mightiest—
       The Wren will prevail— (564)

118.   As we take nature, without permission,
       let us covet you— (565)

119.   The Astounding subjects are the only ones
       we pass unmoved. (568)

120.   The seraphic shame generosity causes
       is perhaps its most heavenly result. (572)

121.   To make even Heaven more heavenly,
       is within the aim of us all. (572)

122.   Devotion should always wear a fence,
       to preempt its claim. (572)

123.   Why the full heart is speechless,
       is one of the great wherefores. (572)

124.   Till it has loved—no man or woman
       can become itself— (575)

125. Death has only to touch a trifle
      to make it portentous— (579)

126. To the faithful Absence is condensed presence.
      To others—but there *are* no others— (587)

127. To die before it feared to die,
      may have been a boon— (596)

128. You spoke of "Hope" surpassing "Home"—
      I thought that Hope *was* Home— (600)

129. To divulge itself is Sorrow's Right—
      never—its presumption. (606)

130. Nature is our eldest mother,
      she will do no harm. (609)

131. Footlights cannot improve the grave,
      only immortality. (610)

132. The water is deeper than the land.
      The swimmer never stagnates. (612)

133. A thousand questions rise to my lips,
      and as suddenly ebb— (619)

134. What indeed is Earth but a Nest,
      from whose rim we are all falling? (619)

135. Earth would not seem homelike without
      your little sunny Acts— (619)

136. Magic, as it electrifies,
      also makes decrepit— (622)

137.   To be singular under plural circumstances,
       is a becoming heroism— (625)

138.   Still as the Profile of a Tree
       against a winter sky. (645)

139.   So valiant is the intimacy
       between Nature and her children. (648)

140.   Great Hungers feed themselves,
       but little Hungers ail in vain. (652)

141.   The pretty boarders are leaving the trees,
       birds and ants and bees. (656)

142.   I am studying music now with the jays,
       and finding them charming artists. (665)

143.   It perished with beautiful reluctance,
       like an evening star— (668)

144.   It may have been she came to show you
       Immortality— (671)

145.   The inferential Knowledge—
       the distinctest one. (685)

146.   *Prudence* is a tedious one,
       and needs beguiling—too— (687)

147.   Genius is the ignition of affection—
       not intellect, as is supposed,— (691)

148.   I know but little of Little Ones,
       but love them very softly— (728)

149.   We read the words but know them not.
       We are too frightened with sorrow. (729)

150.   Heaven is but a little way
       to one who gave it, here. (729)

151.   The mighty dying of my Father
       made no external change— (735)

152.   Home is the riddle of the wise—
       the booty of the dove. (737)

153.   The hearts that never lean, must fall.
       To moan is justified. (742)

154.   Tenderness has not a Date—
       It comes—and overwhelms. (750)

155.   Memory is the Sherry Flower
       Not allowed to wilt— (764)

156.   The friend Anguish reveals is
       the slowest to forget. (788)

157.   I cannot conjecture a form of space
       without her timid face. (790)

158.   Memory is a strange Bell—
       Jubilee, and Knell. (792)

159.   The Port of Peace has many Coves,
       though the main entrance cease. (792)

160.   A Book is only the Heart's Portrait—
       every Page a Pulse— (794)

161. A Blossom perhaps is an introduction,
      to whom—none can infer— (803)

162. I am speechlessly grateful for a friend
      who also was my friend's. (804)

163. What sweeter Shelter than the Hearts
      of such a hallowed Household! (806)

164. Beauty is often timidity—
      perhaps oftener—pain. (807)

165. A Doom of Fruit without the Bloom,
      like the Niger Fig. (814)

166. An hour for books, those enthralling friends,
      the immortalities. (815)

167. "Though thou walk through the Valley of the Shadow of
            Death,
      I will be with thee." (820)

168. We must bring no Twilight
      to one who lost her Dawn— (820)

169. I trust this sweet May Morning
      is not without it's peace (821)

170. Loving the Blest without Abode,
      this too can be learned— (822)

171. Emerson's intimacy with his "Bee"
      only immortalized him— (823)

172. Is not an absent friend as mysterious
      as a bulb in the ground. (824)

173.   How small the furniture of bliss!
       How scant the heavenly fabric! (824)

174.   The Humming Birds and Orioles
       fly by me as I write. (825)

175.   "Yesterday, Today, and Forever,"
       then we will let you go. (829)

176.   That must be a silver bell
       which calls the human heart. (830)

177.   If the future is mighty as the past,
       what may vista be? (830)

178.   Why is it Nobleness makes us ashamed—
       Because it is so seldom or so hallowed? (836)

179.   I wish I might say one liquid word
       to make your sorrow less. (859)

180.   Eat the bit of cake in your garden,
       and let the Robins taste. (863)

181.   And I, consign myself to you
       and find the Nest sufficient— (866)

182.   I cant tell how it is,
       but there *are* influences. (866)

183.   All this and more, though *is* there more?
       More than Love and Death? (873)

184.   Nothing in her Life became her
       like it's last event. (882)

185. I work to drive the awe away,
      yet awe impels the work. (891)

186. Spring's first conviction is a wealth
      beyond its whole experience. (891)

187. The sweetest way I think of you
      is when the day is done. (891)

188. In this place of shafts, I hope
      you may remain unharmed. (892)

189. Icebergs italicize the Sea—
      they do not intercept it. (899)

190. Death cannot plunder half so fast
      as Fervor can re-earn— (901)

191. Choose Flowers that have no Fang, Dear—
      Pang is the Past of Peace— (911)

192. To have been the missing Hero
      is it's own reward— (942)

193. The Thank you in my heart obstructs
      the Thank you on my Lips. (955)

194. Abstinence from Melody
      was what made him die. (968)

195. I cannot depict a friend to my mind
      till I know what he is doing. (969)

196. Biography first convinces us
      of the fleeing of the Biographied— (972)

197. The Amherst Heart is plain and whole
and permanent and warm. (989)

198. To know you better as you flee,
may be our recompense. (989)

199. Tropic, indeed, a memory
that adheres so long. (991)

200. The Honey you went so far to seek,
I trust too you obtain. (1004)

201. Anguish sometimes gives a cause
which was at first concealed. (1006)

202. Dawn and Dew my Bearers be—
Ever, Butterfly. (1013)

203. With closer clutch for that which remains,
for Dying whets the grasp. (1020)

204. It must have been as if he had come
from where dreams are born! (PF 10)

A coda to this chapter might call the reader's attention to the fact that Dickinson developed the same sense of a freed line of poetry that Gerard Manley Hopkins employed. Her line frequently incorporates those extra, unstressed syllables which Hopkins called "outrides" in letters to his friend Bridges. Hopkins used such extra syllables to free his lines from conventional meters. As a result of the extra syllables, his lines seem charged with multiple rhythms. The following fourteener from Dickinson's letter to James D. Clark on the death of the Reverend Charles Wadsworth demonstrates, I believe, the same discovery:

205. His Life was so shy and his tastes so unknown,
that grief for him seems almost unshared. (766)

The two lines seem to read with seven stressed syllables, but the total number of syllables is far beyond fourteen. Another complete poem also shows Dickinson experimenting with sprung rhythm at about the same time as Hopkins:

206. Affection wants you to know it is here.
      Demand it to the utmost. (772)

An epigram in an 1882 letter to Mabel Loomis Todd also contains Hopkins-like outrides:

207. Maturity only enhances mystery,
      never decreases it. (769)

In his 1988 book Kenneth Stocks recorded other similarities between the two poets. Hopkins and Dickinson are two *celibataires* who would have proven poetically congenial.

You asked me if I wrote now?
I have no other Playmate—
Letter 513

Chapter Three

New Poems ·

The second category of new Dickinson works contains poems that look like the short, more familiar poems of her canon. They are complete and finished. They can stand by themselves, free from any context in the letters, as if they had some formal preexistence before Dickinson realized their usefulness for a particular letter. These prose-formatted poems have never been printed as such, nor have they been numbered by Johnson. They are newly discovered and authentic poems by Emily Dickinson that deserve a place in her canon.

The following lines probably should not be judged as poetry. They are too tied to household circumstances, and the form is incomplete. However, the lines suggest the manner in which Dickinson was beginning to experiment with poetic phrasing quite early in her letter-writing career:

Will you forgive me, Susie,
I cannot stay away;
and it is not *me only*—
that writes the note today—
dear Mattie's *heart* is here,
tho' her *hand* is not quite strong enough
to hold a pen today. (70)

Dickinson soon grew stronger as a poet. The following seems to be a poem that is even more fully able to stand on its own:

208.   A small weight—is obnoxious—
upon a weary Rope—
but had you Exile—or Eclipse—
or so huge a Danger,
as would dissolve all other friends—
'twould please me to remain—
Let others—show this Surry's Grace—
Myself—assist his Cross. (277)

Though the poem is complete, the reader may benefit from learning that it was offered in friendship to Samuel Bowles. Dickinson herself formatted the last two lines as poetry by indenting them. Johnson did not print it in the *Complete Poems*, but in the *Letters* he provides the note that Surrey, a prominent lyricist of the English Renaissance, was accused of high treason and beheaded. Thus, the last two lines suggest that others might want to stand by her friend Bowles to share his glory as editor of the Springfield (Mass.) *Republican*, one of the leading newspapers in the country—but she will stand by him when he is suffering.

Dickinson will become still more expert at these prose-formatted letter poems, as she demonstrates in a letter which breaks into a perfect poem in the middle of a sentence:

209.	"the Robins?" They are writing *now*,
	their Desk in every passing Tree,
	but the Magic of Mates that cannot hear them,
	makes their Letters dim— (890)

The first of the famous Master letters provides a complete poem that reads as follows:

210.	The Violets are by my side,
	the Robin very near,
	and "Spring"—they say,
	Who is she—
	going by the door—

	Indeed it is God's house—
	and these are gates of Heaven,
	and to and fro,
	the angels go,
	with their sweet postillions— (187)

The poem follows a progression found in some of Dickinson's other nature poems of the fascicle years: first a simple description of nature and then, in a later stanza, the leap to the transcendental level. In a similar manner, the canonical poem number 130, "These are days when birds come back," leaps from the physical description of Indian summer to a "sacramental" communion with nature.

Letter 435 contains another example of a complete poem, surely one of the best and most thought-provoking additions to the canon:

211.	That a pansy is transitive,
	is its only pang.
	This, precluding that,
	is indeed divine.

If a poem can be a trap for meditation, this is an eminently success-ful example of the genre. It is one of Dickinson's most extraordinary ventures into theological speculation. The reader needs to identify the antecedents of the two pronouns before the poem can finish its extraordinary work. Does it not assert that God and the pansy would be identical, if only the pansy possessed immortality?

These new poems, in fact, contain some of her most daring experiments in thought. In this next poem from letter 689, the crow is almost as miraculous a sign of grace or redemption as the body of Jesus on the cross:

212.   Spring, and not a Blue Bird,
        but I have seen a Crow—
        "in his own Body on the Tree,"
        almost as prima facie—

And the following new poem offers not only one of her profounder insights into human evaluation but also a fine example of her highly experimental rhyming:

213.   It is solemn to remember
        that Vastness—
        is but the Shadow of the Brain
        which casts it— (735)

She is surely the first, perhaps the only poet to fashion the "Vastness" / "casts it" rhyme.

The permeable nature of the barrier between letter and poem is especially apparent during the most highly emotional events. A remarkable example can be found in a letter that Dickinson wrote to her sister-in-law Susan when Susan's child Gilbert died in October 1883. It begins with pentameters but soon breaks into her more recognizable quatrains:

214.   The Vision of Immortal Life has been fulfilled—
        How simply at the last the Fathom comes!
        The Passenger and not the Sea, we find surprises us—

Now my ascended Playmate
must instruct *me*.
Show us, prattling Preceptor,
but the way to thee!

He knew no niggard moment—
his Life was full of Boon—
The Playthings of the Dervish
were not so wild as his—

No crescent was this Creature—
He traveled from the Full—
Such soar, but never set—

I see him in the Star,
and meet his sweet velocity
in everything that flies—

His Life was like the Bugle,
which winds itself away,
his Elegy an echo—
his Requiem ecstasy— (868)

If some of the epithets and reflections seem too weighty for a small
boy, the poem may contain elegiac speculations that relate to other
recent deaths that saddened Dickinson, such as that of the Rever-
end Charles Wadsworth a year and a half earlier. The poem seems
far too perfect to have been written out quickly.

The following is a letter in its entirety, written under the same
circumstances and signed "Emily." It can be formatted as a poem, as
one of her characteristic quatrains:

215.   Perhaps the dear, grieved Heart
         would open to a flower,
         which blesses unrequested,
         and serves without a Sound. (869)

Even Gilbert's last words, in Dickinson's telling, came out as a complete poem, a fourteener:

216.   "Open the Door, open the Door,
         they are waiting for me." (873)

There will always be room for dispute and refinement concerning exactly which lines to choose from the letters. At times the sutures between poetry and prose are almost invisible. The following are offered as lines that Dickinson apparently conceived as poems. They appear without commentary. It might be noted, though, that the third poem from letter 559 below should be added to the growing number of Dickinson's recognized erotic poems: never was a lover invited to bed more charmingly by the beloved.

217.   There is a tall—pale snow storm
         stalking through the fields,
         and bowing here, at my window—
         shant let the fellow in! (176)

218.   Thank God there is a world,
         and that the friends we love
         dwell forever and ever
         in a house above. (179)

219.   Jennie—my Jennie Humphrey—
         I love you well tonight,
         and for a beam from your brown eyes,
         I would give a pearl. (180)

220.   Verily it snows,
         and as descending swans,
         here a pinion and there a pinion,
         and anon a plume,
         come the bright inhabitants
         of the white home. (181)

221.   The summer day on which you came
       and the bees and the south wind,
       seems fabulous as *Heaven* seems
       to a sinful world— (182)

222.   I often wish I was a grass,
       or a toddling daisy,
       whom all these problems of the dust
       might not terrify—

       and should my own machinery
       get slightly out of gear,
       please, kind ladies and gentlemen,
       some one stop the wheel,— (182)

223.   The crumbling elms and evergreens—
       and *other* crumbling things—
       that spring, and fade, and cast their bloom
       within a simple twelvemonth—

       well—*they* are *here*, and skies on me
       fairer far than Italy,
       in blue eye look down—
       up—see!—away—a league from here,
       on the way to Heaven!

       And here are Robins—just got home—
       and giddy Crows—and Jays—
       and will you trust me—as I live,
       here's a *bumblebee*—

       not such as *summer* brings—John—
       earnest, manly bees,
       but a kind of Cockney,
       dressed in jaunty clothes.

Much that is gay—have I to show,
if you were with me, John. (184)

224. If roses had not faded,
and frosts had never come,
and one had not fallen here and there
whom I could not waken,
there were no need of other Heaven
than the one below. (185)

225. I lift the lid to my box of Phantoms,
and lay another in,
unto the Resurrection—
Then will I gather in *Paradise*,
the blossoms fallen here,
and on the shores of the sea of Light,
seek my missing sands. (186)

226. Our man has mown today,
and as he plied his scythe,
I thought of *other* mowings,
and garners far from here. (190)

227. Business enough indeed,
our stately Resurrection!
A special Courtesy, I judge,
from what the Clergy say! (193)

228. Ah! dainty—dainty Death!
Ah! democratic Death!
Grasping the proudest zinnia from my purple garden,—
then deep to his bosom calling the serf's child!
Say, is he everywhere?
Where shall I hide my things? (195)

229.   Complacency! My Father!
       in such a world as this,
       when we must all stand barefoot
       before thy jasper doors! (204)

230.   Am told that fasting gives to food
       marvellous Aroma,
       but by birth a Bachelor,
       disavow Cuisine. (204)

231.   Meeting is well worth parting.
       How kind in some to die,
       adding *impatience* to the rapture
       of our thought of Heaven! (204)

232.   My little Balm might be *o'erlooked*
       by wiser eyes—you know—
       Have you tried the Breeze that swings the Sign—
       or the Hoof of the Dandelion?
       I own 'em—Wait for *mine*! (241)

233.   The Hearts in Amherst—ache—tonight—
       You could not know how hard—
       They thought they could not wait—last night—
       until the Engine—sang—

       a pleasant tune—that time—
       because that you were coming—
       The flowers waited—in the Vase—
       and love got peevish, watching. (259)

234.   The Mind is so near itself—
       it cannot see,
       distinctly— (260)

235.   I often wonder how
       the love of Christ, is done—
       when that—below—
       holds—so— (262)

236.   It is a Suffering, to have a sea—
       no care how Blue—
       between your Soul,
       and you. (272)

237.   That you return to us alive,
       is better than a Summer.
       And more to hear your voice below,
       than News of any Bird. (276)

238.   It was much—that far and ill,
       you recollected me—
       Forgive me if I prize the Grace—
       superior to the Sign. (277)

239.   There lurked a dread that you had gone
       or would seek to go.
       "Where the treasure is,"
       there is the prospective. (313)

240.   My flowers are near and foreign,
       and I have but to cross the floor
       to stand in the Spice Isles. (315)

241.   Travel why to Nature,
       when she dwells with us?
       Those who lift their hats shall see her,
       as devout do God. (321)

242. Busy missing you—
      I have not tasted Spring—
      Should there be other Aprils,
      We will perhaps dine— (324)

243. These Indian-Summer Days
      with their peculiar Peace
      remind me of those stillest things
      that no one can disturb. (332)

244. The mud is very deep—
      up to the wagons' stomachs—
      Arbutus making pink clothes,
      and everything alive.
      Even the hens are touched
      with the things of Bourbon,
      and make republicans like me
      feel strangely out of scene. (339)

245. Life is the finest secret.
      So long as that remains,
      we must all whisper.
      With that sublime exception
      I had no clandestineness. (354)

246. Has All—
      a codicil? (366)

247. Affection is like bread,
      unnoticed till we starve,
      and then we dream of it,
      and sing of it,
      and paint it,
      when every urchin in the street
      has more than he can eat. (379)

248. Now the Grass is Glass
and the Meadow Stucco,
And "Still Waters" in the Pool
where the Frog drinks.

These Behaviors of the Year
hurt almost like Music—
Shifting when it ease us most. (381)

249. A finite life, little sister,
is that peculiar garment
that were it optional with us
we might decline to wear. (385)

250. Spring is a happiness so beautiful,
so unique, so unexpected,
that I don't know what to do with my heart.
I dare not take it,
I dare not leave it—
What do you advise? (389)

251. The mysteries of human nature
surpass the "mysteries of redemption,"
for the infinite we only suppose,
while we see the finite. (389)

252. You are most illustrious
and dwell in Paradise.
I have never believed the latter to be
a superhuman site. (391)

253. Nature gives her love—
Twilight touches Amherst
with his yellow Glove. (392)

254. We remind her we love her—
      Unimportant fact,
      though Dante did'nt think so,
      nor Swift, nor Mirabeau. (393)

255. I always ran Home to Awe when a child,
      if anything befell me.
      He was an awful Mother,
      but I liked him better than none. (405)

256. Death obtains the Rose,
      but the News of Dying goes
      no further than the Breeze.
      The Ear is the last Face. (405)

257. How luscious is the dripping
      of Febuary eaves!
      It makes our thinking Pink—

      It antedates the Robin—
      Bereaving in prospective
      that Febuary leaves— (450)

258. The Ignominy to receive—
      is eased by the reflection
      that interchange of infamies—
      is either's antidote. (467)

259. I dream about father every night,
      always a different dream,
      and forget what I am doing daytimes,
      wondering where he is.
      Without any body, I keep thinking.
      What kind can that be? (471)

260.   The "Happiness" without a cause,
is the best Happiness,
for Glee intuitive and lasting
is the gift of God.

I fear we have all sorrow,
though of different forms—
but with Life so very sweet at the Crisp,
what must it be unfrozen! (472)

261.   I hope you may sometime be
so strong as to smile at now—
That is our Hope's criterion,
for things that are—
are ephemeral,
but those to come—
long— (472)

262.   This is a stern Winter,
and in my Pearl Jail,
I think of Sun and Summer
as visages unknown. (487)

263.   The power to fly is sweet,
though one defer the flying,
as Liberty is Joy,
though never used. (498)

264.   Forgive me if I come too much—
the time to live is frugal—
and good as is a better earth,
it will not quite be this. (498)

265.   "My Country, 'tis of thee,"
has always meant the Woods—to me—
"Sweet Land of Liberty,"
I trust is your own. (509)

266. We must be less than Death,
to be lessened by it—
for nothing is irrevocable
but ourselves. (519)

267. To be human is more than to be divine,
for when Christ was divine,
he was uncontented
till he had been human. (519)

268. The Red Leaves take the Green Leaves place,
and the Landscape yields.
We go to sleep with the Peach in our Hands
and wake with the Stone,
But the Stone is the pledge of Summers to come— (520)

269. Danger is not at first,
for then we are unconscious,
but in the after—slower—Days—

Do not try to be saved—
but let Redemption find you—
as it certainly will—

Love is it's own rescue,
for we—at our supremest,
are but it's trembling Emblems— (522)

270. Accept my timid happiness.
No Joy can be in vain,
but adds to some bright total,
whose Dwelling is unknown— (528)

271. We have no statutes here,
but each does as it will,
which is the sweetest
jurisprudence. (545)

272. Hours—have Wings—
      Riches—have Wings—
      Wings are a mournful perquisite—
      A Society for the Suppression of Wings
      would protect us all. (550)

273. Expulsion from Eden grows indistinct
      in the presence of flowers so blissful,
      and with no disrespect to Genesis,
      Paradise remains. (552)

274. How near this suffering Summer
      are the divine words
      "There is a World elsewhere." (557)

275. I confess that I love him—
      I rejoice that I love him—
      I thank the maker of Heaven and Earth—
      that gave him me to love—

      the exultation floods me.
      I cannot find my channel—
      the Creek turns Sea—
      at thought of thee—
      Will you punish me? (559)

276. Incarcerate me in yourself—
      rosy penalty—
      threading with you this lovely maze,
      which is not Life or Death— (559)

277. We went to sleep as if it were a country—
      let us make it one—
      we could make it one, my native Land—
      my Darling come
      oh *be* a patriot now— (559)

278. It is Anguish I long conceal from you
      to let you leave me, hungry,
      but you ask the divine Crust
      and that would doom the Bread. (562)

279. To see is perhaps never quite the sorcery
      that it is to surmise,
      though the obligation to enchantment
      is always binding—
      It is sweet to recall that we need not retrench,
      as Magic is our most frugal Meal. (565)

280. I fear you have much happiness
      because you spend so much.
      Would adding to it—take it away
      or is that a penurious question? (565)

281. How spacious must be the Heart
      that can include so many,
      and make no error of Love
      toward one— (566)

282. Though we are each unknown to ourself
      and each other,
      'tis not what well conferred it,
      the dying soldier asks,
      it is only the water. (591)

283. Consciousness is the only home
      of which we *now* know.
      That sunny adverb had been enough,
      were it not foreclosed. (591)

284. The only Balmless Wound
      is the departed Human Life
      we had learned to need.

For that, even Immortality
is a slow solace.
All other Peace has many Roots
and will spring again. (597)

285.   Sweet toil for smitten hands
to console the smitten!
Labors as endeared
may engross our lost.
Buds of other days
quivered in remembrance.
Hearts of other days
lent their solemn charm.
Life of flowers lain in flowers—
what a home of dew! (609)

286.   Must I lose the Friend that saved my Life,
without inquiring why?
Affection gropes through Drifts of Awe—
for his Tropic Door—
That every Bliss we know or guess—
hourly befall him—
is his scholar's prayer— (621)

287.   Heaven will not be as good as earth,
unless it bring with it
that sweet power to remember,
which is the Staple of Heaven—here. (623)

288.   I trust you may have the dearest summer
possible to Loss—
One sweet sweet more—One liquid more—
of that Arabian presence! (643)

289. The Weather is like Africa
      and the Flowers like Asia
      And the Numidian Heart of your "Little Friend"
      neither slow nor chill— (650)

290. Neither in Heaven nor Earth,
      have I seen such Beauty.
      Superb as Aurora,
      celestial as Snow. (658)

291. The slips of the last rose of summer
      repose in kindred soil
      with waning bees for mates.
      How softly summer shuts,
      without the creaking of a door,
      abroad for evermore. (669)

292. How sweet the "Life that now is,"
      and how rugged to leave it—
      and ruggeder to stay behind
      when our Dear go— (685)

293. I knew a Bird that would sing as firm
      in the centre of Dissolution,
      as in it's Father's nest—
      Phenix, or the Robin?
      . . . I leave you to guess. (685)

294. The bulbs are in the sod—
      the seeds in homes of paper
      till the sun calls them. (691)

295. We read in a tremendous Book
      about "an enemy,"
      and armed a confidential fort
      to scatter him away.

The time has passed, and years have come,
and yet not any "Satan."
I think he must be making war
upon some other nation. (693)

296.　The little sentences I began
and never finished—
the little wells I dug
and never filled— (748)

297.　The Air is soft as Italy,
but when it touches me,
I spurn it with a Sigh,
because it is not you. (750)

298.　The trespass of my rustic Love
upon your Realms of Ermine,
only a Sovreign could forgive—
I never knelt to other—

The Spirit never twice alike,
but every time another—
That other more divine. Oh,
had I found it sooner! (750)

299.　I know not how to thank you.
We do not thank the Rainbow,
although it's Trophy is a snare.
To give delight is hallowed—
perhaps the toil of Angels,
whose avocations are concealed— (769)

300.　Her dying feels to me
like many kinds of Cold—
at times electric,
at times benumbing—

then a trackless waste,
Love has never trod. (788)

301. "Mother," to me, is so sacred a Name,
I take even that of the "Seraphim"
with less hallowed significance— (789)

302. While others go to Church,
I go to mine,
for are not you my Church,
and have we not a Hymn
that no one knows but us? (790)

303. Those that die seem near me
because I lose my own.
Not *all* my own, thank God,
a darling "own" remains—
more darling than I name. (790)

304. So delicate a diffidence,
how beautiful to see!
I do not think a Girl extant
has so divine a modesty. (790)

305. Nature's faithful Blossoms
whom no one summons but themselves,
Magics of Constancy— (794)

306. The Birds are very bold this Morning,
and sing without a Crumb.
"Meat that we know not of," perhaps,
slily handed them— (820)

307. I have long been a Lunatic on Bulbs,
      though screened by my friends,
      as Lunacy on any theme
      is better undivulged. (823)

308. The withdrawal of the Fuel of Rapture
      does not withdraw the Rapture itself.
      Like Powder in a Drawer,
      We pass it with a Prayer,
      It's Thunders only dormant. (842)

309. Your little mental gallantries
      are sweet as Chivalry,
      which is to me
      a shining Word
      though I dont know its meaning.

      I sometimes remember we are to die,
      and hasten toward the Heart
      which how could I woo
      in a rendezvous
      where there is no Face? (856)

310. Believing that we are to have no Face
      in a farther Life,
      makes the Look of a Friend
      a Boon almost too precious. (859)

311. I am glad you are in the open Air—
      That is nearest Heaven—
      The first Abode "not made with Hands"
      entices to the second— (866)

312. I hesitate which word to take,
      as I can take but few
      and each must be the chiefest,

but recall that Earth's most graphic transaction
is placed within a syllable,
nay, even a gaze— (873)

313.   I saw the Jays this Morning,
each in a Blue Pelisse,
and would have kissed their Lips of Horn,
if I could have caught them,
but Nature took good care! (882)

314.   Trusting the happy flower
will meet you at the Door,
where Spring will soon be knocking,
we challenge your "Come in." (887)

315.   Dear arrears of tenderness
we can never repay
till the will's great ores
are finally sifted;
But bullion is better than minted things,
for it has no alloy. (889)

316.   To have had such Daughters is sanctity—
to have had such a Mother, divine.
To *still* have her, but tears forbid me.
My own is in the Grave.
"So loved her that he died for her,"
says the explaining Jesus. (892)

317.   To be certain we were to meet our Lost,
would be a Vista of reunion,
who of us could bear? (896)

318.   To attempt to speak of what has been,
would be impossible.
Abyss has no Biographer—
Had it, it would not be Abyss. (899)

319. I was with you in all the loneliness,
     when you took your flight,
     for every jostling of the Spirit
     barbs the Loss afresh—
     even the coming out of the Sun
     after an Hour's Rain. (901)

320. Autumn is among us,
     though almost unperceived—
     and the Cricket sings in the morning, now,
     a most pathetic conduct— (936)

321. The Summer has been wide and deep,
     and a deeper Autumn is
     but the Gleam concomitant
     of that waylaying Light— (937)

322. After the great intrusion of Death,
     each one that remains
     has a spectral pricelessness
     besides the mortal worth— (940)

323. The element of Elegy,
     like Bugles at a Grave,
     how solemnly inspiriting! (945)

324. The plants went into camp last night,
     their tender armor insufficient
     for the crafty nights. (948)

325. That we are permanent
     temporarily,
     it is warm to know,
     though we know no more. (962)

326.   How vast is the chastisement of Beauty,
given us by our Maker!
A Word is inundation,
when it comes from the Sea— (965)

327.   Neither fearing Extinction,
nor prizing Redemption,
he believed alone.
Victory was his Rendezvous—
I hope it took him home. (968)

328.   Nothing inclusive of a human Heart
could be "trivial."
That appalling Boon
makes all things paltry but itself— (970)

329.   The Flower keeps it's appointment—
should the Heart be tardy?
When Memory rings her Bell,
let all the Thoughts run in— (973)

330.   Morning without you is a dwindled Dawn—
Quickend toward all celestial things
by Crows I heard this Morning. (981)

331.   To be a Bell and Flower too,
is more than Summer's share,
but Nature is a Partisan— (988)

332.   I hope that you are well,
and nothing mars your peace
but its divinity—
for Ecstasy is peril. (989)

333. "Sweet Land of Liberty"
      is a superfluous Carol
      till it concern ourselves—
      then it outrealms the Birds. (1004)

334. I write in the midst of Sweet-Peas
      and by the side of Orioles,
      and could put my Hand on a Butterfly,
      only he withdraws. (1004)

335. What a Hazard a Letter is!
      When I think of the Hearts it has scuttled and sunk,
      I almost fear to lift my Hand
      to so much as a Superscription. (1007)

336. That your loved Confederate and yourself
      are in ceaseless peace,
      is my happy faith— (1008)

337. Audacity of Bliss, said Jacob to the Angel
      "I will not let thee go
      except I bless thee"—
      Pugilist and Poet, Jacob was correct— (1042)

Riddles are healthful food.
Letter 362

The Riddle that we guess
we speedily despise—
Letter 353

Chapter Four

Tetrameters, Trimeters, Riddles, and Such

In addition to the fourteener epigrams and the other prose-formatted poems found in the letters, still more groups of poems appear there. These poems too are in forms not entirely different from Dickinson's previously acknowledged poems. I have grouped these less frequently used forms as follows: her trimeter poems, her riddles, some other metrical forms, and finally a shadowy group of poems that seem complete but need some hints from the context of the letter for full comprehension. Needless to say, some of these shorter poems demonstrate her epigrammatic style as well as do the fourteeners collected in chapter 2.

Dickinson's earliest poems were trimeter lines: good examples in the *Complete Poems* are numbers 2 to 5. One begins "I have a Bird in spring" (5). She soon expanded her repertoire to include other forms, most often fourteeners, but trimeters continue to appear frequently as fine little epigrams themselves, like the following:

338.　　All we secure of Beauty
　　　　is it's Evanescences— (781)

The unexpected plural of the last word adds Hopkinsian outrides and surprise.

A trimeter epigram from letter 599 reads,

339.　　To come—from Heaven—is casual—
　　　　But to return—eternal.

The arresting word *casual* sends the reader to the dictionary to confirm that Dickinson truly considers our birthings to be "by chance, not planned, purposeless." This single word plunges the poem to the rich religious stratum of her work. Her assertion pulls against the whole weight of the Christian traditions of providence and predestination. The two lines contain all the intellectual riches which made classical epigrams famous and for which Dickinson's poetry too is prized.

Dickinson could fashion her trimeter epigrams in three or more lines also:

340.　　Amalgams are abundant,
　　　　but the lone student of the Mines
　　　　adores Alloyless things— (913)

The subsequent history of this form culminates in the famous verse-unit used in William Carlos Williams's *Paterson* poems of 1946 and after. The following lines, for both their triplet form and the peach, seem worthy precursors:

341. It was so delicious to see you—
      a Peach before the time,
      it makes all seasons possible. (438)

The rest of Dickinson's trimeter epigrams culled from her letters are presented without commentary:

342. The Dust like the Mosquito,
      buzzes round my faith. (235)

343. The Heart wants what it wants—
      or else it does not care— (262)

344. To all except anguish,
      the mind soon adjusts. (311)

345. Where the Treasure is,
      there the Brain is also— (320)

346. There seems a spectral power
      in thought that walks alone. (330)

347. To an Emigrant, Country is idle
      except it be his own. (330)

348. Lifetime is for two,
      never for committee. (343)

349. Enough is so vast a sweetness
      I suppose it never occurs— (352)

350. The quicker deceit dies,
      the better for the truth. (357)

351. Interview is acres,
      while the broadest letter
      feels a bandaged place. (360)

352.   The stimulus of Loss
        makes most Possession mean. (364)

353.   We turn not older with years,
        but newer every day. (379)

354.   To multiply the Harbors
        does not reduce the Sea. (386)

355.   He has had his Future
        who has found Shakespeare— (402)

356.   Presumption has it's Affliction
        as actually as Claim— (429)

357.   That it is true, Master,
        is the Power of all you write. (449)

358.   Labor might fatigue,
        though it is Action's rest. (459)

359.   The Joy we most revere—
        we profane in taking. (477)

360.   I am sorry you need Health,
        but rejoice you do not Affection— (481)

361.   However you stem Nature,
        she at last succeeds. (487)

362.   God seems much more friendly
        through a hearty Lens. (492)

363.   Youth, like Indian Summer,
        comes twice a Year— (502)

364.   I have felt like a troubled Top,
       that spun without reprieve. (525)

365.   Work is a bleak redeemer,
       but it does redeem. (536)

366.   The Grapes were big and fresh,
       tasting like Emerald Dew— (566)

367.   Though but a simple shelter
       I will always last. (567)

368.   To those who can estimate silence,
       it is sweetly enough— (586)

369.   Your coming is a symptom of Summer—
       The Symptom excels the malady. (588)

370.   We cannot believe for each other—
       thought is too sacred a despot. (591)

371.   Gethsemene and Cana
       are still a traveled route. (598)

372.   The cherishing that is speechless,
       is equally warm. (614)

373.   Valor in the dark
       is my Maker's code. (617)

374.   How can we thank each other,
       when omnipotent? (623)

375.   A Spell cannot be tattered,
       and mended like a Coat— (663)

376. Time is short and full,
      like an outgrown Frock— (667)

377. Death goes far around
      to those that want to see him. (670)

378. Sorrow, benighted with Fathoms,
      cannot find it's Mind. (784)

379. Your Gifts are from the Sky,
      more precious than the Birds,
      because more disembodied. (804)

380. To come unto our own
      and our own fail to receive us,
      is a sere response. (815)

381. The ravenousness of fondness
      is best disclosed by children. (824)

382. The angel begins in the morning
      in every human life. (824)

383. When overwhelmed to know,
      I feel that few are sure. (827)

384. The past is not a package
      one can lay away. (830)

385. Night is my favorite Day—
      I love silence so— (843)

386. I hope you may not go—
      That you are near is sinew. (849)

387. Life is so strong a vision,
      not one of it shall fail. (860)

388.   Not what the stars have done,
       but what they are to do,
       is what detains the sky. (860)

389.   The little garden within,
       though tiny, is triumphant. (969)

390.   Who could be ill in March,
       that Month of proclamation? (976)

391.   To know that there is shelter,
       sometimes dissuades it's necessity— (1003)

392.   Who could be motherless
       who has a Mother's Grave
       within confiding reach? (1022)

RIDDLES

Like the fourteener, the riddle is an ancient vernacular form in which—we can confidently state from the evidence of her letters—Dickinson excelled. In many of the examples below the two forms are in fact combined. Her riddles are puzzles that need a clue. Her riddle about the hummingbird, number 1463 in her *Complete Poems*, is famous. Now the list can be greatly expanded.

In one riddle Dickinson offers the reader no help. The following appears in its entirety among her prose fragments in the third volume of her letters. One might venture as an answer "the body," or possibly "the human brain":

393.   Incredible the Lodging
       But limited the Guest. (PF 84)

Or "earth" would fit as well, as would "the heart."
For the rest, clues come from the letters in which they appear.

394. Speculate with all our might,
we cannot ascertain. (332)
(immortality)

395. No event of Wind or Bird
breaks the Spell of Steel.
Nature squanders Rigor—now—
where she squandered Love. (432)
(The answer must be "winter," since she
writes the riddle in January.)

396. She is the Lane to the Indes,
Columbus was looking for. (456)
(George Eliot)

397. We are snatching our jewels from the frost,
and ask you to help us wear them,
as also the trinkets more rotund,
which serve a baser need. (578)
(a gift of flowers and fruit)

398. Night's capacity varies,
but Morning, is inevitable— (616)
(a bad dream)

399. This is but a fragment,
but wholes are not below. (656)
(a letter)

400. To which as to a Reservoir
the smaller Waters go. (833)
(a friend)

401. The gift of neither Heaven nor Earth,
yet coveted of both! (883)
(a friend)

402.   The Organ is moaning—
       the Bells are bowing,
       I ask Vinnie what time it is. (888)
                         (Sunday)

403.   The little package of Ceylon
       arrived in fragrant safety. (889)
                         (tea)

404.   How to repair my shattered ranks
       is a besetting pain. (896)
                   (recent deaths of friends)

405.   The sweet Acclamation of Death divulges it—
       There is no Trumpet like the Tomb— (1043)
                   ("The Might of Human Love")

THE ESSENTIAL CONTEXT

Like unfinished sculptures, some of her poems seem to rest
privately, only half emerged from their relationship to the letter and
its recipient. They require at least some context for their full under-
standing. In a way they are like the riddles above. The reader may
judge whether they belong to her essential canon or not.

The following seems meaningful in itself:

406.   If the anguish of others helped one with one's own,
       now would be many medicines. (298)

But when we know from the context of Dickinson's letter that the
"now" to which she refers is the height of the Civil War, the
fourteener gains immensely.

We know from the letter in which it appears that this set of three
lines memorializes the death of the famous abolitionist Charles
Sumner:

407.	When Continents expire
	The Giants they discarded—are
	Promoted to Endure— (411)

Though Dickinson herself formatted these lines as a poem, John-son did not pick it up for his edition of the poems. It is represen-tative of the many epitaphs, hitherto unnoticed, that Dickinson wrote for famous people.

Dickinson sent a copy of Emerson's *Representative Men* to Hig-ginson's wife as a gift:

408.	I am bringing a little Granite Book
	you can lean upon. (481)

Unfortunately, Higginson misquoted and ridiculed the lines in a letter to his sister, parts of which Johnson includes in a note to letter 481.

Later, when Mrs. Higginson died, Dickinson sent Higginson this fine expression of sympathy:

409.	With sorrow that the Joy is past,
	to make you happy first,
	distrustful of it's Duplicate
	in a hastening World. (516)

The reader needs to know that in the following, Dickinson sym-pathizes with the wife of Samuel Bowles after his death:

410.	To forget you would be impossible,
	had we never seen you;
	for you were his for whom we moan
	while consciousness remains.
	As he was himself Eden,
	he is with Eden,
	for we cannot become what we were not. (567)

And another sympathizes with the death of a cousin's child:

411.   Is his sweet wife too faint to remember
         to Whom her loved one is consigned?
         "Come unto me" could not alarm
         those minute feet— (620)

The letter in which these lines appear seems to chide Higginson's too easy praise of American writers:

412.   Your relentless Music
         dooms as it redeems— (622)

We need to know the poignant context for another poem: the death of her addressee's husband. The addressee was Mrs. Holland, the correspondent for whom Dickinson seemed to have had the most affection. It is a complete poem written as prose:

413.   How sweet that he rose in the morning—
         accompanied by dawn.
         How lovely that he spoke with you,
         that memorial time!
         How gentle that he left the pang
         he had not time to feel!
         Bequest of darkness, yet of light,
         since unborne by him. (732)

These next two lines might be left on their own, as an interesting enigma, though the context shows that Dickinson referred to Judge Lord's *cold*!

414.   Be gentle with it—Coax it—
         Dont drive it or 'twill stay— (750)

In the following it is helpful (though not essential) to know that Dickinson is writing to her sister-in-law Susan next door:

415.   Thank her dear power for having come,
         an Avalanche of Sun! (755)

Sometimes the fourteener is the whole of the letter but lacks some necessary interpretative context. For example, the following, less greeting and signature, was written to the daughter of a neighbor:

416. In a World too full of Beauty for Peace,
I have met nothing more beautiful. (759)

She writes to Mrs. Holland about the recent death of Mrs. Holland's brother, and compares her own dead to those of her friend:

417. Could I visit the Beds
of my own who sleep,
as reprovelessly,
even Night were sweet— (775)

We need to know that another prose-formatted poem was written about a photograph of two newlyweds, one of them never seen before by Dickinson:

418. A lovely Face to sit by
in Life's Mysterious Boat— (802)

The following is obviously poetry, though it helps to know that a family of Dickinson's acquaintance was forced to leave their house one evening because of a flooding and go to a hotel:

419. Baby's flight will embellish History
with Gilpin's and Revere's— (888)

The context also helps to clarify the meaning of the next one and make it more personal:

420. After a brief unconsciousness,
a Sleep that ended with a smile. (890)

The lines refer to Judge Lord's death. And we need to know that the following words refer to the death of a child:

421. Who "meddled" with the costly Hearts
      to which she gave the worth
      and broke them—fearing punishment,
      she ran away from Earth— (893)

The next lines might stand alone, but it extends our knowledge
to know that Dickinson is commenting on "Mark Antony's Oration
over his playmate Caesar":

422. I never knew a broken Heart
      to break itself so sweet— (901)

And commenting on her own collapse, a couple of years before she
died, Dickinson shaped a fourteener even for that event:

423. The doctor calls it "revenge of the nerves";
      but who but Death had wronged them? (907)

To understand the next fourteener, we have to know that its
subject was a forthcoming biography of Samuel Bowles:

424. Like a Memoir of the Sun,
      when the Noon is gone— (908)

The following commented on a family photograph:

425. The picture of the pretty Home
      is very warm and vivid,
      and *we* half "touch" it too,
      unless softly forbidden—
      not with mortal Fingers,
      but those more tidy,
      mental ones,
      which never leave a blot— (925)

The information that Helen Hunt Jackson had recently broken
her leg helps us understand these lines:

426.   I shall watch your passage from Crutch to Cane
       with jealous affection.
       From there to your Wings is but a stride—
       as was said of the convalescing Bird. (937)

The following lines are from a letter commenting on the portrait
of an opera singer:

427.   The brow is that of Deity—
       the eyes, those of the lost,
       but the power lies in the *throat*—
       pleading, sovereign, savage—
       the panther and the dove!
       Each, how innocent! (948)

Dickinson wrote to Charles H. Clark regarding the death of his
brother:

428.   Vivid in our immortal Group
       we still behold your Brother,
       and never hear Northampton Bells
       without saluting him. (963)

In the same letter she also alludes to their deceased mutual friend,
the Reverend Charles Wadsworth, and the kind of time (or eter-
nity) he now enjoys. The lines contain another of her theological
meditations:

429.   Is it a joyous expanse of Year,
       without bisecting Months,
       untiring Anno Domini? (963)

To understand the next lines we have to know that she is sending
thanks for the gift of a book:

430. It stills, incites, infatuates—
blesses and blames in one.
Like Human Affection, we dare not touch it,
yet flee, what else remains? (965)

And it helps the reader to know that in the following she addresses the executor of Judge Lord's estate, though the lines might have a broader applicability:

431. To fulfill the will of a powerless friend
supersedes the Grave. (967)

Here, two lovers are gazing at one another:

432. The voraciousness of that only gaze
and its only return. (969)

The subject here is a girl who had sprained her ankle:

433. Anatomical dishabille
is sweet to those who prize us—
A chastened Grace is twice a Grace.
Nay, 'tis a Holiness. (984)

The subject of this single haunting tetrameter line is Death:

434. We go by detachments to the strange Home. (986)

Perhaps the following is too dependent on the photograph she had apparently received in a recent letter, showing a child on a leopard skin:

435. With Leopards for Playmates, the beautiful Child
defies the Latitudes
and I trust that her Session of Domingo
has but just begun— (1005)

Another fourteener refers to a person who has just died:

436.   To him to whom Events and Omens
        are at last the same. (1006)

And the following prose-formatted poem was addressed to Helen
Hunt Jackson's widower:

437.   Dear friend, can you walk,
        were the last words that I wrote her.
        Dear friend, I can fly—
        her immortal reply. (1015)

    On some occasions the context required is actually not from the
letter but from the expectation that the reader will recall a passage
from the Bible (in this case, from the Gospel of Matthew):

438.   Let the phantom love that enrolls the sparrow
        shield you softer than a child. (609)

In introducing the following prose-formatted fourteener Dickinson
actually put the biblical citation from Proverbs—"Give me thine
Heart"—in quotation marks:

439.   Too peremptory a Courtship for Earth,
        however irresistible in Heaven— (608)

    The second Master letter has already been mentioned as one of
Dickinson's most metrically intense letters. A phrase from that
letter reads:

440.   The prank of the Heart at play on the Heart—
        in holy Holiday. (233)

In the third Master letter the following perfect quatrain appears:

441. Low at the knee that bore her once
      unto wordless rest
      Daisy kneels a culprit—
      tell her her offence. (248)

R. W. Franklin has recently reversed the sequence of these last two
Master letters, much to the improvement of the biographical narra-
tive they contain. But the smaller point here is that intense though
the segments are as poetry, they still beg for some context in a
longer reflective love poem.

There is at least one letter where Dickinson presents an enigma
that not even the context answers:

442. It comforts the Criminal little to know
      that the Law expires with him. (369)

Dickinson gives no hint of what law has been broken and then
repealed.

OTHER POETIC FORMS

Dickinson only rarely wrote pentameters, that high formal line
of the tradition from Shakespeare and Pope to the later Whitman
and beyond. Perhaps it was too public and "patriarchal" a form for
her to feel comfortable with. But her rare pentameters ring nicely
to the ear:

443. That bleeding beginning that every mourner knows. (670)

444. That sweet Physician, an approaching spring— (807)

Glimpses of such lines are rare, as in a letter to Judge Lord where
she compares thoughts of him possibly dying to "the horrid Mon-
sters fled from in a Dream" (752). Only rarely does she venture
upon a run of three pentameters, as on a scrap of paper accompany-
ing flowers:

445. Ferocious as a Bee without a wing
The Prince of Honey and the Prince of Sting
So plain a flower presents her Disk to thee. (739)

Once, under pressure, she broke into urgent dactyls, Virgil's metrical foot in the *Aeneid*:

No one had told me your Sister had died. (866)

Her more natural instinct led her to the fourteener. On one occasion she even recast Shakespeare's pentameter line from *Othello*—"The robb'd that smiles steals something from the thief"—into her characteristic trimeters; in letter 478 she cited the line thus:

446. He that is robbed and smiles,
steals something from the thief.

A form that she used on only a few occasions is the epigram made of a tetrameter couplet:

447. Did she suffer—except to leave you?
That was perhaps the sum of Death— (519)

448. To congratulate the Redeemed is perhaps superfluous
For Redemption leaves nothing for Earth to add— (593)

449. I cannot tell how Eternity seems.
It sweeps around me like a sea. (785)

450. It consoles the happy Sorrow of Autumn,
to know that plumbless ones are near. (945)

451. The Acts of Light which beautified
a Summer now past to it's reward. (951)

452. Had we less to say to those we love,
perhaps we should say it oftener. (962)

Dickinson indented the following tetrameter couplet and format-
ted the lines as a poem, but Johnson did not print it in the *Complete
Poems*:

453. The lovely flowers embarrass me,
      They make me regret I am not a Bee— (1047)

Another form to be found in her letters is quite similar to the
fourteener epigrams of chapter 2. The only difference is that its
lines are reversed: a line of three stresses is followed by a line of four.
Several of these inverted fourteeners are offered below:

454. I have the friend who loves me—
      and thinks me larger than I am— (246)

455. Only Love can wound—
      Only Love assist the Wound. (370)

456. Sweet is it as Life,
      with it's enhancing Shadow of Death. (446)

457. Nature is a Haunted House—
      But Art—a House that tries to be haunted. (459a)

458. "Thank you" ebbs between us,
      but the Basis of thank you, is sterling and fond— (661)

459. There are Sweets of Pathos,
      when Sweets of Mirth have passed away— (668)

460. Fidelity never flickers—
      it is the one unerring Light. (939)

Finally, she produced the following fine dimeter couplets:

461. We meet no Stranger
      but Ourself. (348)

462. Always begins
      by degrees. (470)

463. The Parents of Beauty
      are seldom known— (616)

464. Most of our Moments
      are Moments of Preface— (641)

465. Area—
      no test of depth. (811)

466. A friend is a
      solemnity. (940)

467. Ascension has
      a muffled Route. (945)

468. Changelessness
      is Nature's change. (948)

I'll send you thoughts like daisies,
and sentences could hold the bees.
Letter 301

How lovely are the wiles of Words!
Letter 555

Chapter Five

Workshop Materials

The searcher can establish yet another category of poetic materials in Dickinson's letters—her workshop materials. Such a category might include mere scraps of strikingly figurative phrases like "the Velocity of Affection" (485). In one of the letters, February is called "that Month of fleetest sweetness" (971)—an epithet which in its rhythm, its figurative language, and its internal rhyming surely has many of the elements of poetry. The recording of such brilliant scraps could be almost endless and would cite virtually every page of the three-volume *Letters*.

But the most important category of workshop materials contains the many poems that are *almost* finished—poems in which prosaic lines intrude, or the meter goes dead, or lines seem missing in stanza formations. Some of the pieces in this grouping look like skeletons of possible poems, armatures upon which a future poem might be constructed. Johnson published some of these workshop poems, most notably "Summer—we all have seen—" (1386), with all their variations, in his three-volume variorum edition of the poems.

A good example of this workshop material appears in the following development of a couplet noted earlier, in chapter 2:

469.   There is no first, or last, in Forever—
       It is Centre, there, all the time—
       To believe—is enough,
       and the right of supposing— (288)

The capitalizations and dashes are characteristic of Dickinson's poems; there is a biblical allusion (from Revelation) in the first line and a metaphysical figure of speech in the second. To make it a fully finished poem we might expect one of her characteristic rhymes and perhaps some smoothing out of the rhythm—though many of the works in *Complete Poems* are no more "finished" than this.

The same can be said for the next poem, from a letter written to her mentor Higginson. Not much is needed to fill out the structure and smooth the language. It is a fine example of a poetic armature. For many, it will be poem enough:

470.   Perhaps you smile at me.
       I could not stop for that—
       My Business is Circumference—
       An ignorance, not of Customs,
       but if caught with the Dawn—
       or the Sunset see me—
       Myself the only Kangaroo
       among the Beauty. (268)

In another example from her workshop materials, she has apparently split open a perfect quatrain in order to focus the sentiment for the relative to whom it was written. The quatrain reads as follows:

471.   Summers of bloom—and months of frost,
       and days of jingling bells,
       Today has been so glad without,
       and yet so grieved within— (190)

The intrusive line that splits the stanza in the middle reads, "yet all the while this hand upon our friend"—indicating apparently the sickness of a mutual friend that has made her correspondent sad while external nature was providing reasons for different feelings.

An armature is the framework, made of wire or other materials, upon which a sculpture is built. The following two passages also fit the definition for such workshop pieces:

472.   Were the Velocity of Affection
       as perceptible as it's Sanctity,
       Day and Night
       would be more Affecting. (485)

The piece sounds a bit too much like prosing, as does the next:

473.   There is not so much Life as *talk* of Life,
       as a general thing.
       Had we the first intimation of the Definition of Life,
       the calmest of us would be Lunatics! (492)

One cannot guess where Dickinson would begin to condense these two statements, which seem to lack only compression to become recognizable as her characteristic poems.

The following also looks like the armature for a poem:

474.   That the Divine has been human
       is at first an unheeded solace,
       but it shelters without our consent—

To have lived is a Bliss so powerful—
we must die—to adjust it—
but when you have strength to remember
that Dying dispels nothing which was firm before,
you have avenged sorrow— (523)

The words are a prose sketch for the poem that might develop.
  Another envisioned poem also promises much, had it been am-
plified and sculpted:

475.   Intrusiveness of flowers
       is brooked by even troubled hearts.
       They enter and then knock—
       then chide their ruthless sweetness,
       and then remain forgiven. (540)

  Several lines from a letter struggle for poetic form as they memo-
rialize the deaths of the husband and children of Susan Dickinson's
sister:

476.   A faithful "I am sorry"
       will sometimes save the Heart—
       when every other Savior fails—

       I want to take hold of your Hand
       and tell you that Love lasts—
       though it grows unknown—
       in some dreadful instants—

       We are eternal—dear,
       which seems so worthless, now—
       but will be by and by,
       all we can remember—
       because it owns our own
       and must give them back— (577)

As Rodin might have left armatures for new statues in the studio when he died, so Dickinson left, in her letters, the skeletons for new poems. The following, which I have formatted as possible poetry, is a fine example:

477.　A Promise is firmer than a Hope,
　　　although it does not hold so much—
　　　Hope never knew Horizon—

　　　Awe is the first Hand that is held to us—
　　　Hopelessness in it's first Film
　　　has not the leave to last—

　　　That would close the Spirit,
　　　and no intercession
　　　could do that—

　　　Intimacy with Mystery,
　　　after great Space,
　　　will usurp it's place—

　　　Moving on in the Dark
　　　like Loaded Boats at Night,
　　　though there is no Course,
　　　there is Boundlessness— (871)

Some of the letters, especially to her most intimate correspondents and especially in the most emotionally unsettling circumstances, also seem like poems in the making. The following phrases, for example, are taken in sequence from a letter to the Norcross cousins shortly after the death of Dickinson's mother. They seem to present the rough plan for another fine poem:

478.　Mother's dying almost stunned my spirit. [. . .]
　　　a larger mother died than had she died before. [. . .]
　　　She slipped from our fingers like a flake
　　　gathered by the wind. [. . .]

the grass that received my father
will suffice his guest,
the one he asked at the altar
to visit him all his life. (785)

The following lines seem to me a quatrain lacking a fourth line—
although perhaps they are perfect as is:

479.   Could you tell me how to grow—
        or is it unconveyed—
        like Melody—or Witchcraft? (261)

In fact, many readers will already have come to the conclusion that
a less demanding ear could easily have judged many of these "work-
shop poems" as authentic additions to the first rank of the canon.
Lines from this next letter, for example, come very close to being a
complete and polished poem:

480.   It is very wrong that you were ill,
        and whom shall I accuse?
        The enemy, "eternal, invisible, and full of glory"—
        but He declares himself a friend!

        It is sweet you are better.
        More beating that brave heart has to do
        before the emerald recess. (952)

The following, too, seems like a well-developed sketch for an
impressive poem:

481.   The atmospheric acquaintance
        so recently and delightfully made,
        is not, I trust, ephemeral,
        but absolute as Ether. (953)

The lines below might also be considered one of her complete
poems, even though the meter is rough. If we met them in John-

son's collection of her poetry, we would not hesitate to admire them as one of her typical poems:

482.   The Savior's only signature
        to the Letter he wrote to all mankind,
        was, A Stranger and ye took me in. (1004)

Similarly, is the following to be considered a workshop poem or is it complete?

483.   I have seen one Bird and part of another—
        probably the last,
        for Gibraltar's Feathers would be dismayed
        by this savage Air—
        beautiful, too, ensnaring—
        as Spring always is. (808)

Another apparent workshop poem, written about the recent death of her mother, seems very nearly complete:

484.   Grief of wonder at her fate
        made the winter short,
        and each night I reach
        finds my lungs more breathless,
        seeking what it means. (815)

"Reach" and "means" were often rhyme enough for Dickinson.
     Only a slight intrusive prosing seems to keep the following from being a finished poem, though it could easily stand as the basic plan for a poem:

485.   I fear we think too lightly of
        the gift of mortality,
        which, too gigantic to comprehend,
        certainly cannot be estimated. (524)

Finally, one of her prose fragments contains an overlooked workshop poem in which Dickinson has not yet decided between two alternative lines to give the final shape to a thoughtful quatrain:

486.   Eternity may imitate
        The Affluence (Ecstasy) of time
        But that arrested (suspended) syllable
        is wealthier than him

        But Loves dispelled Emolument
        Finds (Has) no Abode in him—
        (Has no retrieve in him) (PF 24)

I am now very tall
& wear long dresses nearly.
        Letter 13

Chapter Six

Juvenilia, Sources, and the
Growth of the Poet

The letters, when viewed as sources for hitherto unrecognized poems, provide us with many new materials for determining the origins of Dickinson's poetic practice: her juvenilia and the earliest sources in her development as a poet.

JUVENILIA

Among Dickinson's early relationships with young women of her own age, one of the most intense was with Abiah Root. It can be noted here that— with the odd exception of letters to her sister Lavinia—the incidence of poetic materials in Dickinson's letters is, perhaps not surprisingly, the highest where her affections are most engaged.

These cadences appear in a letter to Abiah when Dickinson was twenty-one:

487.   Scatter a fragrant flower
       in this wilderness life of mine. (36)

The following prose-formatted lines are also to Abiah:

488.   I remember the leaves were falling—
       and *now* there are falling snows;
       who maketh the two to differ—
       are not leaves the brethren of snows? (39)

Among her juvenilia is a rhyming valentine which Johnson missed. (Dickinson's first recorded poem in Johnson's edition of the *Complete Poems* is a mock valentine of 1850.) Some context is needed for the present valentine. Dickinson made and sent a lamp-mat to the young man who received the letter:

489.   *I* weave for the Lamp of *Evening*—
       but fairer colors than *mine*
       are twined while stars are shining.
       I know of a shuttle swift—
       I know of a fairy gift—
       mat for the "Lamp of *Life*"—
       the little Bachelor's wife! (41)

Even at age 21, Dickinson was beginning to frame prose-formatted poems. The following lines, in fact, approach her later epigrammatic style; they stand easily alone:

490.   These brief imperfect meetings
       have a tale to tell. (50)

So also do the following lines, plodding but with her recognizable cadences, found later in the same letter:

491. Her thot's tho' they are *older*
have all the charm of youth—
have not yet lost their freshness,
their innocence and peace—

she seems so pure in heart—
so sunny and serene,
like some sweet Lark or Robin
ever soaring and singing—

I have not seen her much—
I want to see her more—

Still later, toward the end of the same letter, more incipient poetry emerges:

492. Oh there is much to speak of
in meeting one you love.

And finally, the very last lines of this intense letter seem to aspire toward scansion also:

493. Writing is brief and fleeting—
conversation will come again,
yet if it *will*, it hastes
and must be on it's way—
earth is short Abiah,
but Paradise is *long*
there must be many moments
in an eternal day—
then *sometime we* shall tarry,
while time and tide *roll on*,
and till then Vale!

Dickinson's brother Austin was also the object of her intense affection. One finds a striking poetic phrase in an early letter to him (she is 21):

494.   It's evening and the orchestra of winds
        perform their strange, sad music. (60)

She was also deeply attached to Susan Gilbert, who would become Austin's wife. One of the earliest prose-formatted poems appears in a letter to her:

495.   Who loves you most,
        and loves you best,
        and thinks of you
        when others rest?
        T'is Emilie— (77)

I remember seeing lyrics like this flashing by the car window when I was a boy; they ended with the name of a widely used item of male toiletry. Genius was hardly needed to produce such a rhyme, but it shows how close Dickinson's prose was to the cadences of poetry.

In a letter to Austin dated 27 March 1853 (when Dickinson was 23 years old) she banters with him about their both being poets. The letter contains another early prose-formatted letter poem. It is obviously not of the quality of the later productions, but it signals her early steps in the genre:

496.   Austin is a Poet, Austin writes a psalm.
        Out of the way, Pegasus,
        Olympus enough "to him,"
        and just say to those "nine muses"
        that we have done with them!
        Raised a living muse ourselves,
        worth the whole nine of them.
        Up, off, tramp!

She continues to "Brother Pegasus," that "I've been in the habit *myself* of writing some few things" (110). Her instrument is by no means fully tuned, but she does begin consciously to take on the identity of a poet.

Dickinson wrote a playful poem to her cousin John Graves in

1853. She formatted it as poetry, but Johnson did not include it in the *Complete Poems.*

497.   A little poem we will write unto our Cousin John,
       to tell him if he does not come and see us very soon,
       we will immediately forget there's any such a man,
       and when he comes to see us, we will not be "at home."

(117)

Dickinson wrote the following prose-formatted poem in a letter when she was visiting in Washington, D.C. Addressed to Susan, it shows another step toward her more mature style:

498.   Sweet and soft as summer, Darlings,
       maple trees in bloom. [. . .]
       hardly seems it possible
       this is winter still;
       and it makes the grass spring
       in this heart of mine
       and each linnet sing,
       to think that you have come.
       Dear Children—Mattie—Sue—
       for one look at you,
       for your gentle voices,
       I'd exchange it all.
       The pomp—the court—the etiquette—
       they are of the earth—
       will not enter heaven. (178)

SOURCES

The models Dickinson admired in her youth may seem rather conventional and unsurprising to modern readers, but they place her among the avant-garde of her time. She wrote the following to her brother Austin, away at law school in Cambridge. The year was 1853 and Dickinson was in her early twenties.

"would some power the giftie gie" folks, to see themselves as we see them. Burns. I have read the poems, Austin, and am going to read them again, and will hand them to Susie— They please me very much, but I must read them again before I know just [what] I think of "Alexander *Smith*"— They are not very coherent, but there's good deal of exquisite frensy, and some wonderful figures, as ever I met in my life—We will talk about it again— (128)

She shows her acquaintance with Robert Burns here and mentions him in other letters, as well as imitating him on several occasions: letters 180 and 184, for example, contain prose-formatted poems, printed elsewhere in this book, that are modeled on "John Anderson, My Jo." It was Burns who had helped to restore the popularity of the fourteener (the older ballad form) in such songs as "O My Love's like a red, red rose," "Bonnie Doon," and his more discursive "Address to the Unco Guid." In earlier letters Dickinson had actually cited "John Anderson my Joe [*sic*]" (99) and "Auld Lang syne" (111). Burns is surely one source of her fourteeners.

More surprising in the letter cited above is the name of Alexander Smith (1830–67), a poet highly regarded at the time. He would later be satirized as a member of the "Spasmodic School" (and in letter 265 Dickinson would complain to Higginson, "You think my gait 'spasmodic' "), but he was much prized and imitated by Tennyson, among other notables, for his excited verse and his passion for political freedom. His line of choice was a rather awkward pentameter, but his themes were meditative and philosophical. These remarks on Smith are the most extended discussion of a writer to be found in Dickinson's letters.

From the testimony of the letters, we know that she also knew Tennyson well and admired him. Some of the songs in "Maud" and in "The Princess"—which Dickinson mentions reading when she was about eighteen years old (letter 23)—are skillful fourteeners. Among other writers she mentions in the letters, Byron was also expert with the fourteener. Additional sources for Dickinson's fourteener have recently been documented in books by Benjamin Lease and Judy Jo Small, and I have mentioned others in an earlier chapter.

These writers and the long, partly anonymous tradition of balladeers and hymn writers seem to have created in Dickinson a sense of the fourteener as a natural cadence for writing. Indeed, this study illustrates that she heard fourteeners even in prose, especially when she wanted to be emphatic or memorable. Her famous refusal of Higginson's invitation to come to Boston is a good example:

> I do not cross my Father's ground
> to any House or town. (330)

Her equally famous exclamation at seeing the photograph of Samuel Bowles—

> You have the most triumphant Face
> out of Paradise— (489)

is also a fourteener.

Some of her seemingly casual fourteeners are almost poems, almost worthy to cull and place among her epigrams. To Maria Whitney, who was vacationing in the countryside, she wrote:

> Has Nature won you away from us,
> as we feared she would? (948)

Not all of these fourteeners are of proverb quality. One of them, written to Mrs. Holland, reads,

> You always were a Wren, you know,
> the tenant of a Twig— (950)

and to Mrs. Sweetser:

> We miss you more this time, I think,
> than all the times before— (951)

In a letter probably written to a relative and reflecting on her mother's death, Dickinson wrote,

> I know you will remember her
> with never ceasing love— (800).

Dickinson's instinct for the fourteener was so deep and constant that she frequently started a letter with one:

> The thoughtfulness was picturesque
> and the glimpse delightful— (706)

The technique is most visible in the careful letters to her friend Mrs. Holland, a large percentage of which open with a fourteener. These surely do not rise to the level of poetry, but they amply demonstrate Dickinson's cadence of choice even in prose. The following are some examples of letters to Mrs. Holland which begin with four-teeners:

> I have a fear I did not thank you
> for the thoughtful Candy. (359)

> I once more come, with my little Load—
> Is it too heavy, Sister? (475)

> I have felt so sweet an impatience to write you,
> that I thought it perhaps inordinate. (487)

> I miss my little Sanctuary
> and her redeeming ways. (521)

> Your sweet Face alighted in the Rain,
> with it's Smile unharmed— (542)

> I have thought of you with confiding Love,
> but to speak seemed taken from me— (792)

It was sweet to touch the familiar Hand
that so long had led us— (820)

When Dickinson received a telegram announcing the death of Mrs.
Holland's husband, she started her letter:

We read the words but know them not.
We are too frightened with sorrow. (729)

Her following letter begins similarly:

Panting to help the dear ones
and yet not knowing how,

and soon breaks into poetry (formatted as prose):

if I can rest them,
here is down—
or rescue,
here is power. (730)

Another letter in this bereavement series to Mrs. Holland also
expresses her sympathy in lines that can read as a fourteener:

No solitude receives him,
but neighborhood and friend. (732)

Dickinson sometimes begins *and ends* letters to Mrs. Holland
with fourteeners, as in the following:

We wont fatigue the Fairy Scribe
with a farther Letter. [. . .]

Commending the Birds of which I spoke,
to your Hearts and Crumbs.
                    (808; see also 792 and 806)

She begins a letter to Charles Clark with a fourteener:

> The sorrowful tidings of your Note
> almost dissuade reply. (818)

A letter to the Norcross cousins contains a fourteener that can *almost* stand on its own as a poem:

> —Love for the glad if you know them,
> for the sad if they know you. (382)

Even some of Dickinson's most prosaic materials fall into fourteeners, as when she thanked her sister-in-law's sister Martha for a thoughtful gift:

> It was like my Mattie to send the Peaches,
> pink as the Heart they indorse— (654)

A letter to Susan next door comments on her little boy's tricks:

> Your Urchin is more antique in wiles
> than the Egyptian Sphinx— (664)

With one of her constant fourteeners she wishes Mrs. Sweetser and her family well:

> a wish that would almost be a Prayer,
> were Emily not a Pagan— (566)

In fact, she not infrequently writes in fourteeners as her ordinary prose style:

> I hope you were well since we knew of you,
> and as happy as Sorrow would allow— (668)

Even commenting on the daily news to Mrs. Holland—on the health of the president—she cannot keep from breaking out in fourteeners:

> The Pilgrim's Empire seems to stoop—
> I hope it will not fall— (721)

And a thank-you note for some bulbs opens with a fourteener:

> The Snow will guide the Hyacinths
> to where their Mates are sleeping. (885)

I do not claim these last examples as new poems. But there is no dispute that the signature line of Emily Dickinson's poetry is the fourteener. And Dickinson's tendency to use the same rhythm and meter for her prose indicates that the line between her poetry and prose is not entirely fixed.

The Amherst Heart is plain and whole
and permanent and warm.
Letter 989

Chapter Seven
Bibliographical Essay

When the first collection of Dickinson's letters appeared in 1894, one of the reviewers remarked of them that "not a shell, but contains its pearl. There are phrases that are poems in epitome" (quoted in Wider, 20). But until now, Dickinson's letters have been used by critics mainly to build their own versions of her profile as a writer. The works of Knapp, Leder, Stonum, and Lease can be mentioned in this connection, though most other critics have also mined the letters in this way. Richard Sewall and Cynthia Griffin Wolff, among others, have used the letters to great advantage for biographical details.

Much of the writing on Dickinson's letters has hitherto focused on their subject matter, or their portrayal of Dickinson's developing consciousness, or her ways of appealing to and manipulating the different recipients of the letters. Janet Buell's essay in the *New England Quarterly*, for example, is a fine discussion of the topic of death in Dickinson's letters, particularly those written during the bereavement-filled last decade of her life. She writes with empathy: "Dickinson's form of spinsterhood required courage. . . . She determined to explore immortality in the wider circumference of virginal solitude" (326). Vivian Pollak, in her 1969 dissertation, was most interested in the letters' subject matter and the developing "private" style of Dickinson's earliest correspondence. The variety of subjects in the letters also prompted May Swenson to write an appreciative essay in 1985.

Sylvia Shurbutt's 1979 essay explored the letters (as well as the poems) for evidence that Dickinson found the tropes of "Royalty" useful in expressing her own growing self-consciousness and self-awareness. In her famous *American Literature* article, Heather Thomas used some of the letters to build the case for Dickinson's anorexia. Lillian Faderman's equally famous essay in the *Massachusetts Review* cited a wide range of Dickinson's letters to women for evidence of her homoerotic or homosocial temperament. Suzanne Juhasz divided her 1984 essay in a way that proved especially productive. Exploring the possibility that all of Dickinson's letters were "seductive" in one way or another, she divided her study according to the major recipients of the letters—Dickinson's brother Austin, his wife Susan, the mentor Higginson, the friend Mrs. Holland—and she established for each a particular "gestalt of affection and need" (185). The result was a mosaic of poses by which Dickinson defined herself to her correspondents—and which also provides the only way that the modern reader can know the poet who managed all of these different stances in the solitary room of the writer.

But until now no critic has fully developed or acknowledged the implications of a perception that has been present in the critical literature for many decades: the recognition that there are undeniable poetic qualities in Dickinson's prose letters. Johnson suggested the nature of the task when he introduced the letters initially, writing that "both in style and rhythm [they] begin to take on qualities that are so nearly the quality of her poems as on occasion to leave the reader in doubt where the letter leaves off and the poem begins" (*Letters*, 1.xv). The hint was passed along and kept alive, toyed with from a distance in several later works on Dickinson. In chapter 5 of his 1968 dissertation, Robert Lambert began a discussion of fragmentary poems in Dickinson's letters, calling them "semi-stanzas" or "semi-poetry." He believed, though, that these fourteeners disappear from her letters after the 1860s. In 1979 Sharon Cameron referred to the letters as "metrical compositions that . . . share characteristic features of the poems" (12), though she did not discuss the letters themselves in any detail. Martha Nell Smith's 1985 dissertation is a detailed study of Dickinson's letters as a highly controlled form of self-publication in which she carefully tailored individual letters to their actual recipients. Smith is particularly interested in the different ways that Dickinson addressed her male and female correspondents. In discussing one of the Master letters, Smith mentioned "how Dickinson weaves poems into her prose" and suggested that critics "ponder Dickinson's designs in blending poetry with prose and blurring the distinctions between them" (20 and 22). In 1987 Cristanne Miller noted a few "metered phrases" (11) that appear in the Dickinson letters. In 1990 Judy Jo Small studied the "music" of the poetry—its rhythms, rhymes, and subtle sounds—but did not pursue her considerations in an examination of the letters. In a recently published essay, Sarah Wider comes very close to my own conclusions: "Since the poems in Dickinson's letters contain multiple references and speak to multiple audiences, it comes as little surprise that the same poem often appeared in different letters. By themselves, these poems are markedly without personal reference. . . . The poems could readily be taken out of one context and introduced into another" (28). But she goes on to state her preference for leaving the poems in their letter contexts.

The most lively statement of this position is in a recent essay by Paula Bennett (1992), in which she attacks Thomas H. Johnson for the editorial principles which lead him to "reduce" Dickinson's handwritten words to the conventions of printing. Bennett chides Johnson for "imposing closure" on Dickinson by casting her poems into print, where she "resisted . . . closure" by her subtle experimentings, especially with different kinds of spacing. She attacks Johnson's practice of quoting poems from the letters even when Dickinson herself had written the lines as poetry. It is true that reproductions of any work of art will always lag behind the reality of the originals. But Bennett's position seems to make all methods of printing Dickinson's writings problematic if not impossible.

Finally, Judith Farr has kept the issue alive with the following remarks in her 1992 book, *The Passion of Emily Dickinson*: "Writing letters that scan, enclosing poems in letters, composing poems that are letters, revising and rerevising both, Dickinson did not always sharply distinguish between the uses of her art" (16). The present study is thus the next logical step in a long tradition of critical insight.

Dickinson was always the self-publisher of her poems. Her unconventional formatting methods hid many of her best poems from us until we were ready to listen more closely to the cadences of her letters. These latent poems allow us to see even more of "a soul at the white heat." They confirm for us a writer witty, wise, and meditative, one who has won spiritual truths from solitude. With their calm wisdom they confirm again her links to the Transcendentalist tradition and make her clearly an embodiment of the American Sophia. They add to the delight of the general reader as well as to that of the scholar. Both will search these new poems for a still more complete picture of the Poet.

Bibliography

Abrams, M. H. *A Glossary of Literary Terms*. 5th ed. New York: Holt, Rinehart and Winston, 1988.

Bennett, Paula. *Emily Dickinson: Woman Poet*. Iowa City: University of Iowa Press, 1990.

———. " 'By a Mouth That Cannot Speak': Spectral Presence in Emily Dickinson's Letters." *Emily Dickinson Journal* 1, no. 2 (1992): 76–99.

Buell, Janet W. " 'A Slow Solace': Emily Dickinson and Consolation." *New England Quarterly* 62, no. 3 (September 1989): 323–45.

Cameron, Sharon. *Lyric Time: Dickinson and the Limits of Genre*. Baltimore: Johns Hopkins University Press, 1979.

Dickinson, Emily. *The Complete Poems of Emily Dickinson*. Edited by Thomas H. Johnson. Boston: Little, Brown, 1960.

———. *The Letters of Emily Dickinson*. Edited by Thomas H. Johnson. 3 vols. Cambridge: Harvard University Press, 1958.

———. *The Master Letters of Emily Dickinson*. Edited by R. W. Franklin. Amherst, Mass.: Amherst College Press, 1986.

———. *The Poems of Emily Dickinson*. Edited by Thomas H. Johnson. 3 vols. Cambridge: Harvard University Press, 1955.

Eberwein, Jane. *Dickinson: Strategies of Limitation*. Amherst: University of Massachusetts Press, 1985.

Faderman, Lillian. "Emily Dickinson's Letters to Sue Gilbert." *Massachusetts Review* 18 (1975): 197–225.

Farr, Judith. *The Passion of Emily Dickinson*. Cambridge: Harvard University Press, 1992.

Firbank, P. N. "A Double Life." *New York Review of Books*, 25 June 1992, 3–6.

Franklin, R. W. *The Editing of Emily Dickinson: A Reconsideration*. Madison: University of Wisconsin Press, 1967.

Holman, C. Hugh. *A Handbook to Literature*. 3d ed. Indianapolis: Odyssey Press, 1972.

Hudson, Hoyt Hopewell. *The Epigram in the English Renaissance.*
Princeton: Princeton University Press, 1947.

Juhasz, Suzanne. "Reading Emily Dickinson's Letters." *ESQ: A Journal of the American Renaissance* 30, no. 3 (1984): 170–92.

Knapp, Bettina L. *Emily Dickinson.* New York: Continuum, 1989.

Lambert, Robert Graham, Jr. *The Prose of a Poet: A Critical Study of Emily Dickinson's Letters.* Ph.D. diss., University of Pittsburgh, 1968.

Lease, Benjamin. *Emily Dickinson's Readings of Men and Books: Sacred Soundings.* New York: St. Martin's Press, 1990.

Leder, Sharon, with Andrea Abbott. *The Language of Exclusion: The Poetry of Emily Dickinson and Christina Rossetti.* New York: Greenwood Press, 1987.

Lucas, Dolores Dyer. *Emily Dickinson and Riddle.* DeKalb: Northern Illinois University Press, 1969.

McGann, Jerome J. *The Beauty of Inflections: Literary Investigations in Historical Method and Theory.* Oxford: Clarendon Press, 1985.

———. *The Textual Condition.* Princeton: Princeton University Press, 1991.

McKinstry, S. Jaret. " 'How Lovely are the Wiles of Words!' — or, 'Subjects Hinder talk': The Letters of Emily Dickinson." In *Engendering the Word*, edited by Temma Berg et al., pp. 193–207. Urbana: University of Illinois Press, 1989.

Mann, John. "Dickinson's Letters to Higginson." In *Approaches to Teaching Dickinson's Poetry*, edited by Robin Riley Fast and Christine Mack Gordon, pp. 39–46. New York: Modern Language Association of America, 1989.

Mieder, Wolfgang, with Stewart A. Kingsbury and Kelsie B. Harder. *A Dictionary of American Proverbs.* New York: Oxford University Press, 1991.

Miller, Cristanne. " 'A Letter is a Joy of Earth': Dickinson's Communication with the World." *Legacy* 3, no. 1 (Spring 1986): 29–39.

———. *Emily Dickinson: A Poet's Grammar.* Cambridge: Harvard University Press, 1987.

Nixon, Paul. *Martial and the Modern Epigram.* New York: Longmans, Green, 1927.

Pollak, Vivian R. *Emily Dickinson's Early Poems and Letters*. Ph.D. diss., Brandeis University, 1969.

Sewall, Richard B. *The Life of Emily Dickinson*. 2 vols. New York: Farrar, Straus and Giroux, 1974.

Shurbutt, Sylvia Bailey. "A Developing Self as Revealed through the Royalty Imagery in the Poems and Letters of Emily Dickinson." *American Transcendental Quarterly* 42 (1979): 167–76.

Shurr, William H. *The Marriage of Emily Dickinson: A Study of the Fascicles*. Lexington: University Press of Kentucky, 1983.

Small, Judy Jo. *Positive as Sound: Emily Dickinson's Rhyme*. Athens: University of Georgia Press, 1990.

Smith, Martha Nell. *"Rowing in Eden": Gender and the Poetics of Emily Dickinson*. Ph.D. diss., Rutgers University, 1985.

Stocks, Kenneth. *Emily Dickinson and the Modern Consciousness*. London: Macmillan, 1988.

Stonum, Gary Lee. *The Dickinson Sublime*. Madison: University of Wisconsin Press, 1990.

Swenson, May. " 'Big My Secret, But It's Bandaged.' " *Parnassus* 12–13, no. 2–1 (1985): 16–44.

Thomas, Heather Kirk. "Emily Dickinson's 'Renunciation' and Anorexia Nervosa." *American Literature* 60, no. 2 (May 1988): 205–25.

Walsh, John Evangelist. *This Brief Tragedy: Unraveling the Todd-Dickinson Affair*. New York: Grove Weidenfeld, 1991.

Whipple, Thomas King. *Martial and the English Epigram*. Berkeley: University of California Press, 1925.

White, Jon Manchip. *A Journeying Boy*. New York: Atlantic Monthly Press, 1991.

Wider, Sarah. "Corresponding Worlds: The Art of Emily Dickinson's Letters." *Emily Dickinson Journal* 1, no. 1 (1992): 19–38.

Williams, William Procter, and Craig S. Abbott. *An Introduction to Bibliographical and Textual Studies*. New York: Modern Language Association of America, 1985.

Wolff, Cynthia Griffin. *Emily Dickinson*. New York: Knopf, 1987.

Index of Subjects

Abrams, M. H., 15
American Sophia, 106
American writers, 74
Amherst, 8
"Angel in the house": Victorian
notion of, 20
Anorexia, 104
Antony, Mark: oration over
Caesar, 76
Aphorism, 14
Armature, 84, 85, 86, 88

Balladeers, 98. See also Fourteener
Ballad meter. See Fourteener
Bennett, Paula, 105–6
Bereavement series, 100
Bible, 19, 79; Psalms, 17, 18;
Proverbs, 17, 18, 79; Isaiah, 18;
Matthew, 79; Revelation, 85
Blake, William, 11
Boston, 98
Bowles, Samuel, 9, 39, 76, 98
Bowles, Mrs. Samuel (Mary
Schermerhorn), 73
Bradstreet, Anne: and
"Meditations Divine and
Morall," 19
Buell, Janet, 103
Burns, Robert, 97
Byron, George Gordon, Lord, 97

Cameron, Sharon, 105
Canon, 1, 2, 5, 10, 11, 12, 38, 40, 72,
89
Civil War, 72
Clark, Charles H., 77, 101

Clark, James D., 7, 36
Classical tradition: epigram in, 19,
65
Coleridge, Samuel, 17
"Common measure." See
Fourteener
Context: missing from poem, 72–
80

Dactyl, 81
Death: poems and letters on, 20,
36, 41, 42, 72, 73, 74, 75, 79, 80,
87, 90, 99, 100, 103. See also
Epitaphs
Dickinson, Austin, 94, 95, 96, 97,
104
Dickinson, Emily: epigrammatic
style, 64, 93; on her own
collapse, 76; identity as poet,
95
Dickinson, Lavinia, 92
Dickinson, Susan Gilbert, 5, 6, 7,
8, 9, 41, 74, 95, 96, 97, 101, 104
Dickinson, Thomas Gilbert, 41, 43
Dimeter couplets, 82

Elegiac speculations, 42
Eliot, George, 71
Emerson, Ralph Waldo: and
Representative Men, 73
Epigrams, 2, 6, 10, 12, 14–19, 65,
81, 98; trimeter, 8, 64, 65–66, 81;
as aphorisms, 14; fourteener,
14–21, 64, 82; English, 16, 19; in
classical tradition, 19, 65. See
also Fourteener

Epitaphs, 73; elegiac speculations, 42; and expressions of sympathy, 73, 100; bereavement series, 100. *See also* Death

Epithet, 42, 84

Erotic poems, 43; seductive quality of poems, 104

Experimental rhyming, 41

Faderman, Lillian, 104

Farr, Judith, 106

Fascicles, 11, 40

Figurative language, 15, 84

Fourteener, 3, 5, 8, 36, 43, 64, 65, 70, 72, 75, 76, 79, 81, 97, 98, 99, 100, 101, 105; common measure, 3; hymn meter, 3, 15; ballad meter, 3, 97. *See also* Epigram

Franklin, Benjamin: and Poor Richard, 18, 19

Franklin, R. W., 80

Gilbert, Martha Isabella (Mattie), 87, 96, 101

Gilbert, Susan. *See* Dickinson, Susan Gilbert

Graves, John, 95

Greek Anthology, 15

H.D. (Hilda Doolittle), 15

Harington, Sir John, 16

Higginson, Thomas Wentworth, 7, 8, 19, 73, 74, 85, 97, 98, 104

Higginson, Mrs. Thomas Wentworth (Mary Potter Thacher), 6, 73

Holland, Elizabeth, 5, 6, 74, 75, 98, 99, 100, 102, 104

Holman, C. Hugh, 17

Homoerotic temperament, 104

Hopkins, Gerard Manley, 36–37; and outrides, 36, 37, 65

Hunt, William S. (Helen Hunt's widower), 79

Hymn meter. *See* Fourteener

Hymn writers, 98. *See also* Fourteener

Immortality, 41, 71; and theological speculations, 40, 77

Intimate correspondents, 88; women as, 92; and homoerotic temperament, 104

Isaiah. *See* Bible

Jackson, Helen Hunt, 4, 9, 76

Jesus, 41

Johnson, Thomas H., 1, 2, 3–4, 5, 6, 7, 8, 9, 15, 18, 19, 21, 38, 39, 73, 82, 84, 89, 93, 96, 104, 105; *The Complete Poems of Emily Dickinson,* 2, 5, 6, 9, 10, 19, 39, 65, 70, 82, 85, 93, 96; *The Letters of Emily Dickinson,* 39, 84

Jonson, Ben, 16

Juhasz, Suzanne, 104

Juvenilia, 2, 92–96

Knapp, Bettina, 103

Lambert, Robert, 105

Landor, Walter Savage, 16

Latin tradition: Martial and, 15

Lease, Benjamin, 97, 103

Leder, Sharon, 103

Lord, Otis Phillips (Judge), 74, 80; death of, 75; and executor, 78

Lowth, Robert, 17; and *The Sacred Poetry of the Hebrews,* 17

McGann, Jerome, 11–12

Martial: and the Latin tradition, 15

Master letters, 19, 40, 79, 80, 105

Matthew. *See* Bible

Meditations, theological, 77
Metaphysical: figures of speech, 85
Metrics: of the letters, 1–13
Miller, Cristanne, 9, 105
Models: and sources, 2, 92, 96

Nature, 86; in poems, 40
Norcross, Louise and Frances, 20, 88, 101

Outrides: of Hopkins, 36, 37, 65
Owen, John, 16

Patriarchy: and poetic form, 80
Pentameters, 80, 81, 97
Phelps, Susan Davis, 18
Pollak, Vivian, 104
Poor Richard (Franklin), 18, 19
Pope, Alexander, 16, 80
Predestination, 65
Prior, Matthew, 17
"Private" style: of Dickinson's
    letters, 104
Prose fragments, 15, 18, 91
Proverbs. See Bible
Providence, 65
Psalms. See Bible

Quatrains, 5, 7, 41, 42, 79, 85, 89, 91

Revelation. See Bible
Riddles, 2, 64, 70, 72
Rochester, Lord (John Wilmot), 15–16
Rodin, 88
Root, Abiah, 92, 93
"Royalty": tropes of, 104

Seductive quality of poems, 104; erotic poems, 43

Self-publication, 105, 106
Sewall, Richard B.: Dickinson
    biography, 1, 103
Shakespeare, William, 80; and
    Othello, 81
Shurbutt, Sylvia, 104
Shurr, William H.: The Marriage of
    Emily Dickinson, 11
Small, Judy Jo, 97, 105
Smith, Alexander, 97
Smith, Martha Nell, 105
Sources: for Dickinson, 2, 92; and
    models, 96
Spasmodic School, 97
Stocks, Kenneth, 37
Stonum, Gary Lee, 103
Sumner, Charles, 72
Surrey, Henry Howard, 39
Sweetser, Cornelia Peck, 98, 101
Swenson, May, 104
Sympathy, expressions of, 73, 100

Tennyson, Alfred Lord, 97
Tetrameters, 81, 82
Theological speculations, 40; and
    meditation, 40; and
    immortality, 41, 71; and
    theological meditations, 77
Thomas, Heather, 104
Todd, Mabel Loomis, 37
Transcendental, 40; and the
    Transcendentalist tradition, 106
Trimeters. See Epigram

Valentine, 93
Virgil: and the Aeneid, 81

Wadsworth, Reverend Charles, 7, 36, 42, 77
Washington, D.C., 96
White, Jon Manchip, 16

Whitman, Walt, 80
Whitney, Maria, 98
Wider, Sarah, 105
Williams, William Carlos: and
Paterson, 65
Wilmot, John, Earl of Rochester,
15–16

Wolff, Cynthia Griffin, 9, 103
Women: as intimate
correspondents, 88;
relationships with, 92; and
homoerotic temperament, 104
Workshop materials, 2, 84–91; as
armature, 84, 85, 86, 88

Index of First Lines

The numbers in parentheses
denote the poem numbers used
in this volume; the appropriate
page numbers follow. The exact
punctuation or capitalization of
the lines as they appear in the text
is not necessarily duplicated here.

A blossom perhaps is an
  introduction (161), 33
A book is only the heart's portrait
  (160), 32
A doom of fruit without the
  bloom (165), 33
A faithful "I am sorry" (476), 87
A finite life, little sister (249), 49
A friend is a (466), 83
A letter always seemed to me (3),
  7
A little poem we will write unto
  our cousin John (497), 96
A lovely face to sit by (418), 75
A promise is firmer than a hope
  (477), 88
A small weight—is obnoxious
  (208), 39
A spell cannot be tattered (375), 68
A thousand questions rise to my
  lips (133), 30
Abstinence from melody (194), 35
Accept my timid happiness (270),
  52
Adulation is inexpensive (109), 28
Affection is like bread (247), 48
Affection wants you to know it is
  here (206), 37

After a brief unconsciousness
  (420), 75
After the great intrusion of death
  (322), 61
Ah! dainty—dainty death! (228),
  45
All this and more, though is there
  more (183), 34
All we secure of beauty (338), 65
Always begins (462), 83
Am told that fasting gives to food
  (230), 46
Amalgams are abundant (340), 65
Amazing human heart (4), 7
Amazing human heart (5), 8
An hour for books, those
  enthralling friends (166), 33
Anatomical dishabille (433), 78
And I, consign myself to you
  (181), 34
Anguish sometimes gives a cause
  (201), 36
Area (465), 83
As we take nature, without
  permission (118), 29
Ascension has (467), 83
Audacity of bliss, said Jacob to the
  angel (337), 63
Austin is a poet, Austin writes a
  psalm (496), 95
Autumn is among us (320), 61
Awkward as the homely are (49),
  23

Baby's flight will embellish
  history (419), 75

Be gentle with it—coax it (414), 74

Beauty is often timidity (164), 33

Believing that we are to have no face (310), 59

Biography first convinces us (196), 35

Business enough indeed (227), 45

Busy missing you (242), 48

Cages—do not suit the Swiss— (31), 22

Changelessness (468), 83

Choose flowers that have no fang, dear (191), 35

Complacency! my father (229), 46

Consciousness is the only home (283), 54

Consummation is the hurry of fools (12), 18

Could I visit the beds (417), 75

Could you tell me how to grow (479), 89

Danger is not at first (269), 52

Dawn and dew my bearers be (202), 36

Dear arrears of tenderness (315), 60

Dear friend, can you walk (437), 79

Dear Mr Bowles found out too late (110), 28

Death cannot plunder half so fast (190), 35

Death goes far around (377), 69

Death has only to touch a trifle (125), 30

Death is perhaps an intimate friend (97), 27

Death obtains the rose (256), 50

Delight has no competitor (65), 25

Devotion should always wear a fence (122), 29

Did she suffer—except to leave you (447), 81

Dying is a wild night (54), 24

Earth would not seem homelike without (135), 30

Eat the bit of cake in your garden (180), 34

Emerson's intimacy with his "bee" (171), 33

Enough is so vast a sweetness (349), 66

Eternity may imitate (486), 91

Expulsion from Eden grows indistinct (273), 53

Fear—like dying, dilates trust (88), 26

Ferocious as a bee without a wing (445), 81

Fidelity never flickers (460), 82

Footlights cannot improve the grave (131), 30

For the comprehension of suffering (81), 26

Forgive me if I come too much (264), 51

Friends are nations in themselves (40), 22

Genius is the ignition of affection (147), 31

Gethsemene and Cana (371), 68

Gibraltar's feathers would be dismayed (483), 90

God seems much more friendly (362), 67

Good times are always mutual (93), 27

Gratitude is the timid wealth (52), 23

Great hungers feed themselves (140), 31

Grief of wonder at her fate (484), 90

Had I a pleasure you had not (37), 22

Had we less to say to those we love (452), 81

Had you an hour unengrossed (82), 26

Has all (246), 48

He has had his future (355), 67

He that is robbed and smiles (446), 81

Heaven is but a little way (150), 32

Heaven will not be as good as earth (287), 55

Her dying feels to me (300), 57

Her reluctances are sweeter (98), 27

Her thot's tho' they are older (491), 94

Hereafter, I will pick no rose (24), 21

His life was so shy and his tastes so unknown (205), 36

Home is so far from home (9), 9

Home is the riddle of the wise (152), 32

Home itself is far from home (8), 9

Hours—have wings (272), 53

How can we thank each other (374), 68

How lonesome to be an article (63), 24

How lovely that he spoke with you (413), 74

How luscious is the dripping (257), 50

How near this suffering summer (274), 53

How precious thought and speech are (104), 28

How small the furniture of bliss (173), 34

How spacious must be the heart (281), 54

How strange that nature does not knock (101), 28

How sweet the "life that now is" (292), 56

How to repair my shattered ranks (404), 72

How vast is the chastisement of beauty (326), 62

However you stem nature (361), 67

I always ran home to awe when a child (255), 50

I am bringing a little granite book (408), 73

I am glad you are in the open air (311), 59

I am sorry you need health (360), 67

I am speechlessly grateful for a friend (162), 33

I am studying music now with the jays (142), 31

I am sure I feel as Noah did (42), 23

I cannot conjecture a form of space (157), 32

I cannot depict a friend to my mind (195), 35

I cannot tell how eternity seems (449), 81

I cant tell how it is (182), 34

I confess that I love him (275), 53

I could not weigh myself—myself (33), 22

I dream about father every night (259), 50

I fear we think too lightly of (485), 90

I fear you have much happiness (280), 54

I had hoped to express more (43), 23

I have felt like a troubled top (364), 68

I have long been a lunatic on bulbs (307), 59

I have the friend who loves me (454), 82

I hesitate which word to take (312), 59

I hope that you are well (332), 62

I hope you are joyful frequently (100), 27

I hope you may not go (386), 69

I hope you may sometime be (261), 51

I hope your rambles have been sweet (113), 29

I knew a bird that would sing as firm (293), 56

I know but little of little ones (148), 31

I know not how to thank you (299), 57

I lift the lid to my box of phantoms (225), 45

I never knew a broken heart (422), 76

I notice where death has been introduced (45), 23

I often wish I was a grass (222), 44

I often wonder how (235), 47

I raise only robins on my farm (89), 27

I remember the leaves were falling (488), 93

I remember your coming as serious sweetness (61), 24

I saw the jays this morning (313), 60

I shall watch your passage from crutch to cane (426), 77

I think it sad to have a friend (32), 22

I thought that being a poem one's self (79), 26

I thought to shun the loneliness (77), 26

I thought your approbation fame (99), 27

I trust this sweet May morning (169), 33

I trust you may have the dearest summer (288), 55

I was with you in all the loneliness (319), 61

I weave for the lamp of evening (489), 93

I wish I might say one liquid word (179), 34

I wish one could be sure the suffering (34), 22

I work to drive the awe away (185), 35

I write in the midst of sweet-peas (334), 63

Icebergs italicize the sea (189), 35

If roses had not faded (224), 45

If the anguish of others (406), 72

If the future is mighty as the past (177), 34

In a world too full of beauty for peace (416), 75

In this place of shafts, I hope
(188), 35
Incarcerate me in yourself (276),
53
Incredible the lodging (393), 70
Interview is acres (351), 66
Intrusiveness of flowers (475),
87
Is his sweet wife too faint to
remember (411), 74
Is it a joyous expanse of year
(429), 77
Is it intellect that the patriot
means (19), 20
Is not an absent friend as
mysterious (172), 33
Is not the distinction of affection
(105), 28
Is this the hope that opens and
shuts (6), 8
It comforts the criminal little to
know (442), 80
It consoles the happy sorrow of
autumn (450), 81
It is a suffering, to have a sea
(236), 47
It is anguish I long conceal from
you (278), 54
It is delicate that each mind is
itself (90), 27
It is easier to look behind at a pain
(38), 22
It is of realms unratified (95), 27
It is solemn to remember (213), 41
It is still as distinct as paradise
(91), 27
It is the meek that valor wear (73),
25
It is very wrong that you were ill
(480), 89
It may have been she came to
show you (144), 31

It must have been as if he had
come (204), 36
It perished with beautiful
reluctance (143), 31
It stills, incites, infatuates (430), 78
It was much—that far and ill
(238), 47
It was so delicious to see you
(341), 66
It's evening and the orchestra of
winds (494), 95
It's fragrant news, to know they
pine (36), 22

Jennie—my Jennie Humphrey
(219), 43

Labor might fatigue (358), 67
Landscapes reverence the frost
(60), 24
Let the phantom love that enrolls
the sparrow (438), 79
Life is death we're lengthy at (41),
23
Life is so strong a vision (387), 69
Life is the finest secret (245), 48
Lifetime is for two (348), 66
Like a memoir of the sun (424), 76
Love is that one perfect labor (66),
25
Loving the blest without abode
(170), 33
Low at the knee that bore her
once (441), 80

Magic, as it electrifies (136), 30
Many an angel, with its needle
(18), 20
Many can boast a hollyhock (27),
21
Maturity only enhances mystery
(207), 37

Meeting is well worth parting
(231), 46
Memory is a strange bell (158), 32
Memory is the sherry flower (155),
32
Morning without you is a
dwindled dawn (330), 62
Most of our moments (464), 83
"Mother," to me, is so sacred a
name (301), 58
Mother's dying almost stunned
my spirit (478), 88
Must I lose the friend that saved
my life (286), 55
"My country, 'tis of thee" (265), 51
My family of apparitions (86), 26
My flowers are near and foreign
(240), 47
My life has been too simple and
stern (53), 24
My little balm might be
o'erlooked (232), 46

Nature gives her love (253), 49
Nature is a haunted house (457),
82
Nature is our eldest mother (130),
30
Nature must be too young to feel
(85), 26
Nature, seems it to myself (46), 23
Nature's faithful blossoms (305),
58
Neither fearing extinction (327),
62
Neither in heaven nor earth (290),
56
Night is my favorite day (385), 69
Night's capacity varies (398), 71
No event of wind or bird (395), 71
No heart that broke but further
went (72), 25

No rose, yet felt myself a'bloom
(14), 19
Not a flake assaults my birds (50),
23
Not all of life to live, is it (21), 21
Not what the stars have done
(388), 70
Nothing in her life became her
(184), 34
Nothing inclusive of a human
heart (328), 62
November always seemed to me
(44), 23
Now the grass is glass (248), 49

Oh matchless earth—we
underrate (59), 24
Oh there is much to speak of
(492), 94
Only love can wound (455), 82
Open the door, open the door
(216), 43
Our man has mown today (226),
45

Parting is one of the exactions
(11), 12
Perhaps the dear, grieved heart
(215), 42
Perhaps you smile at me (470), 85
Please rest the life so many own
(84), 26
Presumption has it's affliction
(356), 67
Prudence is a tedious one (146),
31

Save me from the idolatry (115), 29
Scatter a fragrant flower (487), 93
Science will not trust us (76), 25
She is the lane to the Indes (396),
71

She talked of you before she went (1), 5

Show me eternity, and I will show you memory (10), 10

Silence' oblation to the ear (92), 27

So delicate a diffidence (304), 58

So valiant is the intimacy (139), 31

Some time is longer than the rest (25), 21

Sorrow almost resents love (107), 28

Sorrow, benighted with fathoms (378), 69

Speculate with all our might (394), 71

Spring, and not a blue bird (212), 41

Spring is a happiness so beautiful (250), 49

Spring's first conviction is a wealth (186), 35

Still as the profile of a tree (138), 31

Success is dust, but an aim (17), 20

Summers of bloom—and months of frost (471), 86

Sweet and soft as summer, darlings (498), 96

Sweet is it as life (456), 82

"Sweet land of liberty" (333), 63

Sweet toil for smitten hands (285), 55

Tenderness has not a date (154), 32

Thank God there is a world (218), 43

Thank her dear power for having come (415), 74

"Thank you" ebbs between us (458), 82

That a pansy is transitive (211), 40

That bareheaded life—under the grass (28), 21

That bleeding beginning that every mourner knows (443), 80

That it is true, master (357), 67

That must be a silver bell (176), 34

That possession fairest lies (68), 25

That sorrow dare to touch the loved (116), 29

That sweet physician, an approaching spring (444), 80

That the divine has been human (474), 86

That we are permanent (325), 61

That you return to us alive (237), 47

That your loved confederate and yourself (336), 63

The acts of light which beautified (451), 81

The air is soft as Italy (297), 57

The Amherst heart is plain and whole (197), 36

The angel begins in the morning (382), 69

The astounding subjects are the only ones (119), 29

The atmospheric acquaintance (481), 89

The bird would be a soundless thing (55), 24

The birds are very bold this morning (306), 58

The blood is more showy (gaudy) than the breath (20), 21

The brow is that of deity (427), 77

The bulbs are in the sod (294), 56

The career of flowers differs from ours (75), 25

The cherishing that is speechless (372), 68

The crumbling elms and
evergreens (223), 44
The doctor calls it "revenge of the
nerves" (423), 76
The dust like a mosquito (342), 66
The element of elegy (323), 61
The flower keeps it's
appointment (329), 62
The friend anguish reveals is (156),
32
The gift of neither heaven nor
earth (401), 71
The grapes were big and fresh
(366), 68
The "happiness" without a cause
(260), 51
The heart is the only workman
(39), 22
The heart wants what it wants
(343), 66
The hearts in Amherst—ache—
tonight (233), 46
The hearts that never lean, must
fall (153), 32
The honey you went so far to
seek (200), 36
The humming birds and orioles
(174), 34
The ignominy to receive (258),
50
The immortality of flowers (106),
28
The incredible never surprises us
(58), 24
The inferential knowledge (145),
31
The "infinite beauty"—of which
you speak (47), 23
The joy we most revere (359), 67
The little garden within (389), 70
The little package of Ceylon (403),
72
The little sentences I began (296),
57
The love of God may be taught
(29), 22
The love which comes without
aspect (111), 28
The lovely flowers embarrass me
(453), 82
The mighty dying of my father
(151), 32
The mind is so near itself (234), 46
The minor toys of the year are
alike (78), 26
The mud is very deep (244), 48
The mysteries of human nature
(251), 49
The only balmless wound (284),
54
The organ is moaning (402), 72
The parents of beauty (463), 83
The past is not a package (384), 69
The picture of the pretty home
(425), 76
The plants went into camp last
night (324), 61
The port of peace has many coves
(159), 32
The power to fly is sweet (263), 51
The prank of the heart at play on
the heart (440), 79
The pretty boarders are leaving
the trees (141), 31
The quicker deceit dies (350), 66
The ravenousness of fondness
(381), 69
The red leaves take the green
leaves place (268), 52
The risks of immortality (62), 24
"The robins?" They are writing
now (209), 40
The sailor cannot see the north
(35), 22

The savior's only signature (482), 90

The seraphic shame generosity causes (120), 29

The slips of the last rose of summer (291), 56

The soul must go by death alone (48), 23

The stimulus of loss (352), 67

The summer day on which you came (221), 44

The summer has been wide and deep (321), 61

The sweet acclamation of death divulges it (405), 72

The sweetest way I think of you (187), 35

The thank you in my heart obstructs (193), 35

The things of which we want the proof (56), 24

The tiniest ones are the mightiest (117), 29

The trespass of my rustic love (298), 57

The unknown is the largest need (94), 27

The violets are by my side (210), 40

The vision of immortal life has been fulfilled (214), 41

The voraciousness of that only gaze (432), 78

The water is deeper than the land (132), 30

The weather is like Africa (289), 56

The will is always near, dear (70), 25

The withdrawal of the fuel of rapture (308), 59

Then will I not repine (2), 6

There are sweets of pathos (459), 82

There is a tall—pale snow storm (217), 43

There is no first, or last, in forever (15), 20

There is no first, or last, in forever (469), 85

There is not so much life as talk of life (473), 86

There is nothing sweeter than honor, but love (87), 26

There lurked a dread that you had gone (239), 47

There seems a spectral power (346), 66

These brief imperfect meetings (490), 93

These Indian-Summer days (243), 48

"They say that absence conquers" (22), 21

Think of that great courageous place (51), 23

This is a stern winter (262), 51

This is but a fragment (399), 71

This is the world that opens and shuts (7), 8

"This tabernacle" is a blissful trial (112), 28

Those that die seem near me (303), 58

Though but a simple shelter (367), 68

Though thou walk through the valley (167), 33

Though we are each unknown to ourself (282), 54

Till it has loved—no man or woman (124), 29

Time is short and full (376), 69

To all except anguish (344), 66

To an emigrant, country is idle
(347), 66
To attempt to speak of what has
been (318), 60
To be a bell and flower too (331),
62
To be certain we were to meet
our lost (317), 60
To be human is more than to be
divine (267), 52
To be singular under plural
circumstances (137), 31
To come—from heaven—is casual
(339), 65
To come unto our own (380), 69
To congratulate the redeemed is
perhaps superfluous (448), 81
To die before it feared to die (127),
30
To divulge itself is sorrow's right
(129), 30
To forget you would be
impossible (410), 73
To fulfill the will of a powerless
friend (431), 78
To have been the missing hero
(192), 35
To have had such daughters is
sanctity (316), 60
To him to whom events and
omens (436), 79
To know that there is shelter
(391), 70
To know you better as you flee
(198), 36
To live lasts always, but to love
(71), 25
To make even heaven more
heavenly (121), 29
To multiply the harbors (354), 67
To see is perhaps never quite the
sorcery (279), 54

To the faithful absence is
condensed presence (126), 30
To those who can estimate
silence (368), 68
To which as to a reservoir (400),
71
Too peremptory a courtship for
earth (439), 79
Transport's mighty price is (69),
25
Travel why to nature (241), 47
Trial as a stimulus (83), 26
Tropic, indeed, a memory (199),
36
Trusting the happy flower (314),
60

Valor in the dark (373), 68
Verily it snows (220), 43
Vivid in our immortal group
(428), 77

We all have moments with the
dust (16), 20
We are snatching our jewels from
the frost (397), 71
We cannot believe for each other
(370), 68
We go by detachments to the
strange home (434), 78
We have no statutes here (271), 52
We meet no stranger (461), 82
We must be careful what we say
(74), 25
We must be less than death (266),
52
We must bring no twilight (168),
33
We read in a tremendous book
(295), 56
We read the words but know
them not (149), 32

We remind her we love her (254), 50

"We thank thee oh father" for these strange minds (96), 27

We turn not older with years (353), 67

We went to sleep as if it were a country (277), 53

We would'nt mind the sun, dear (26), 21

Were the velocity of affection (472), 86

What a hazard a letter is (335), 63

What indeed is earth but a nest (134), 30

What miracles the news is (64), 24

What sweeter shelter than the hearts (163), 33

Whatever await us of doom or home (114), 29

When continents expire (407), 73

When overwhelmed to know (383), 69

When thou goest through the waters (13), 18

Where the treasure is (345), 66

Where we owe so much it defies money (108), 28

While others go to church (302), 58

Who could be ill in March (390), 70

Who could be motherless (392), 70

Who knows how deep the heart is (57), 24

Who knows where our hearts go (23), 21

Who loves you most (495), 95

Who "meddled" with the costly hearts (421), 76

Why is it nobleness makes us ashamed (178), 34

Why the full heart is speechless (123), 29

Why the thief ingredient (67), 25

With closer clutch for that which remains (203), 36

With leopards for playmates, the beautiful child (435), 78

With sorrow that the joy is past (409), 73

Work is a bleak redeemer (365), 68

Writing is brief and fleeting (493), 94

"Yesterday, today, and forever" (175), 34

You are most illustrious (252), 49

You asked me if I wrote now (102), 28

You have experienced sanctity (80), 26

You might not know I remembered you (30), 22

You see we keep a jealous heart (103), 28

You spoke of "hope" surpassing "home" (128), 30

Your coming is a symptom of summer (369), 68

Your gifts are from the sky (379), 69

Your little mental gallantries (309), 59

Your relentless music (412), 74

Youth, like Indian Summer (363), 67

Library of Congress Cataloging-in-Publication Data

Dickinson, Emily, 1830–1886.

New poems of Emily Dickinson / edited by William H. Shurr with Anna

Dunlap and Emily Grey Shurr.

p. cm.

Includes bibliographical references and indexes.

ISBN 0-8078-2115-2 (hard : alk. paper). — ISBN 0-8078-4416-0 (pbk. : alk. paper)

1. Dickinson, Emily, 1830–1886—Criticism, Textual. 2. Dickinson, Emily, 1830–

1886—Correspondence. 3. Canon (Literature) 4. Literary form. I. Shurr, William.

II. Title.

PS1541.A6   1993b

811'.4—dc20   93-20353

CIP